In a brief compass, Lindsay Brown helpfully encapsulates the nature of the missionary impetus of the Reformation. It has been often maintained that Reformers like Luther and Calvin were not interested in missions. Nothing could be further from the truth. Despite their spatial limitations and geographical context, their labours – fueled by a conviction of the pressing need to re-evangelize Europe – were distinctly missional. Brown also considers the way in which Luther and Calvin also sought to bring the truth of Christianity to all spheres of human life, a helpful reminder that Christ lays claim to the totality of life.

Michael A. G. Haykin
Chair and Professor of Church History, The Southern
Baptist Theological Seminary, Louisville, Kentucky

Lindsay Brown gives readers a simple yet profound look into the missionary heart of both Luther and Calvin. While certainly concerned with evangelism, their's was a much more encompassing vision of the gospel: God's glory extended to the ends of the earth. For those looking to understand and imbibe this Reformation vision, let Brown be your guide.

Coleman M. Ford
Co-founder of the Center for Ancient Christian Studies,
Adjunct Instructor of Church History, Boyce College,
Louisville, Kentucky

Superb! That was my response after reading the book's thrilling content describing and applying the profound legacy of reformers like Luther and Calvin on the Western world and beyond. Key doctrines 'long forgotten' were rediscovered and the author explains helpfully the significance of the Five Solas and the Lordship of Christ before outlining ways in which Luther and Calvin applied biblical principles to the whole of life and society. Calvin's renewed vision for mission and evangelism with his strategic thinking and initiatives for the advance of the gospel provide an urgent challenge for Christians today. The final chapter with its 'Ten Lessons for Today' is essential reading for any involved in church leadership and evangelism. You will benefit immensely from reading this book.

Eryl Davies
Former pastor and Principal; Research Supervisor,
Union School of Theology, Bridgend
and Elder at Heath Church, Cardiff

INTO ALL THE WORLD

The Missionary Vision of Luther and Calvin

LINDSAY BROWN

CHRISTIAN
FOCUS

Copyright © Lindsay Brown 2021

paperback ISBN 978-1-5271-0422-8
epub ISBN 978-1-5271-0714-4
mobi 978-1-5271-0715-1

Published in 2021 by
Christian Focus Publications Ltd,
Geanies House, Fearn, Ross-shire,
IV20 1TW, Scotland
www.christianfocus.com

A CIP catalogue record for this book is
available from the British Library.

Cover design by Rubner Durais

Printed and bound by Gutenberg

CONTENTS

This book is dedicated to Mansell Richards, who first introduced me to the Reformation and is the finest history teacher I have known.

Author's Preface

Why yet another book on the Reformation? After all, there are so many. True, but to my mind most of the books written by historians and theologians about Calvin and Luther over the years have focussed on their contribution to reforming the church and recovering the essence of the Christian Gospel. Such an emphasis is appropriate because of the enormous impact their teachings had on the understanding and growth of the Christian Church and its Gospel around the world in the last 500 years. However, it is my contention in this small book that they should be applauded, in addition, for their contribution in two other areas.

First, the Reformation of European culture. Luther and Calvin not only 'rediscovered' the Christian Gospel which had been clouded in accretions of centuries of Roman Catholic tradition, but they also contributed to the reshaping of European culture as they, and their disciples, attempted to apply Biblical truth to the whole of society, including the world of education, the sciences, the arts, politics, human freedom, and so much more. It really is impossible to understand modern Europe and indeed the western world without recognising the impact of their teaching.

Secondly, for centuries it has been fashionable amongst historians to decry their apparent lack of missionary vision. However, in recent decades a new body of church historians has attempted to reevaluate their missionary vision by re-reading texts of the sermons and commentaries carefully and observing the impact which their teaching, beginning in Wittenberg and Geneva, had on the whole Continent. In the last thirty years historians in Europe such as Alister McGrath in Oxford, Jean-Marc Berthoud and Andy Buckler in France, Scott Simmons and Michael Haykin in the US, Torsten Prill in Africa and Robert Woodberry in Singapore, have all done fresh research and groundbreaking work on the missiology of both Reformers. In this short book I have only sought to allude to their writings and collate some of their findings. I hope you will find it helpful.

In this task I have been wonderfully assisted by Heather Capper, my cheerful and servant-spirited PA, Julia Cameron and Colin Duriez, two highly competent editors and the editorial and graphic team at Christian Focus. They have only sought to clarify and improve the text, so any historical errors, omissions or inconsistencies in the text are sadly only mine, not theirs. I hope you will be able to look beyond any such errors and enjoy and be inspired by the teachings of these two great reformers. Anyone looking for fresh inspiration related to the renewal and re-energising of the church in Europe would do well to ask what lessons we can learn from the ministry and lives of these two men.

Lindsay Brown
November 2020

Introduction

The sixteenth-century Reformation was the spiritual equivalent of a tsunami. It brought enormous spiritual changes across Europe, and affected the political, economic and social landscape in unexpected ways. Its chief architects were Martin Luther, the great German reformer who initiated the Reformation by pinning his 95 theses to a church door in Wittenberg, and John Calvin, the French theologian. Calvin developed and deepened the impact of Luther's biblical convictions across a large part of the continent. Through his legacy, as we shall see, this influence would reach into other parts of the world.

It is fashionable these days to play down the importance of historical reflection. Henry Ford – the founder of the Ford Motor Car company – was famously quoted as saying, 'History is bunk'.[1] Friedrich Hegel (1770-1831), the German philosopher, reputedly protested that the lesson of history is that it teaches us nothing.

---

1. *New York Times*, 29 October, 1921.

The Christian faith is an historical faith, rooted in God's acts in history. This is not just empirical fact, but it bears on each of us personally. John Lennox, an Oxford Professor of Mathematics, once said to me, 'If we don't understand where we've come from, we won't know who we are, and we certainly won't know where we're going.' In other words, an historical perspective is crucial to our identity.

Martin Luther himself is said to have remarked that there is nothing so short as the Christian's memory! Many problems occur in our lives because of a lack of historical perspective, and our failure to absorb the lessons of history. The Apostle Peter, writing to Christians dispersed around the ancient world, urged they should remember not to forget.[2] This urging from the Apostle sums up my reason for writing this book.

THE LEGACY OF THE REFORMATION

The Reformation had a defining and far-reaching impact on the western world and beyond. It shaped the development of Europe over the next five hundred years. It not only touched on key doctrinal issues, but had wide implications for society and for the shaping of culture.

It brought a clear theology of work and vocation, and created a bridge across the secular and sacred divide. It shaped economic thinking, and brought the expansion of education in general, and the university system in particular. The birth of liberal democracy came out of the Reformation, as did religious tolerance. Its new hymnody would revive church worship. More, the

---

2. See 2 Peter 1:12-15.

Reformation brought a fresh perspective on the visual arts, and on how the world of science should relate to faith. This all evolved as a result of Calvin's and Luther's missionary vision.

In the final chapter are ten areas of the Reformers' legacy which merit reflection today.

First, we look back carefully, to help ourselves look forward clearly.

RECOVERING THE ESSENCE OF THE GOSPEL

1

REDISCOVERING BIBLICAL TRUTH

The Reformers were not communicating a new message. They were simply re-emphasising, and perhaps to some extent re-discovering, the teachings embedded in Scripture. The essence of the gospel had been commonly taught in the early church, but it had become lost in the secretions of Roman Catholic teaching.

Luther and Calvin had their precursors in two earlier giants: John Wycliffe (c. 1320s-1384), often known as 'the Morning Star of the Reformation', who taught similar truths in England; and Jan Hus (1372-1415) who was burnt at the stake almost exactly a hundred years before Luther pinned his theses to the Wittenberg church door. So when Luther and Calvin sought to open up the clear teaching of Scripture, they saw themselves as building on the legacy of others. Luther himself said, 'We teach no new thing; we repeat and establish all things which the Apostles and all godly teachers have taught before us.'[1]

---

1. Luther, *Commentary on the Apostle Paul's Letter to the Galatians* (1:4a), quoted in Michael Reeves and John Stott, *The Reformation:*

John Jewel, the Bishop of Salisbury, underlined this when he wrote, 'We bring you nothing but what the Apostles and Christ our Saviour brought before us.'[2] Bishop Lancelot Andrewes (1555-1626), who was head translator of what became known as the King James Bible, asserted aptly, 'We are not innovators, but renovators'.[3] In other words, they were reaffirming the teachings of the early church—which had been encrusted by the traditions of the Roman Catholic Church over the centuries, and to which additions had been made over the generations.

THE HISTORY OF THE TERM 'EVANGELICAL'

It is sometimes implied that the word 'evangelical' dates back only to the sixteenth century, as if the evangelical movement had begun as a sectarian reaction to the monolith of the Roman Catholic Church.

The word was used as far back as the second century in debates with the early heretic Marcion (around A.D. 180) to describe those whose aspiration was to be faithful to the New Testament text. The first-century believers held to the apostolic teaching regarding the authority of Scripture and Christ's deity, death and physical resurrection. They also believed in God's act of justifying those whom He brought to salvation, through Christ's death. These were the hallmarks of the New Testament church.

What You Need to Know and Why (Hendrickson Publishers, Lausanne Library, 2017).

2. *Ibid.*, pp. 33, 34.

3. *Ibid.*, p. 34.

So the word 'evangelical' predates the creation of both the Eastern Orthodox and Roman Catholic churches. It derives from '*euangelion*', a Greek word which the Bible translator William Tyndale (1494-1536) described as 'good and merry, glad tidings which makes a man's heart glad, and makes him sing, dance and leap for joy'.[4]

What the Reformers Re-discovered

What was it that Luther and Calvin re-discovered? Their teaching was rooted in three long-forgotten and neglected cornerstones of New Testament Christianity, namely:

- The doctrine of justification by grace through faith.

- The acceptance of Scripture rather than church tradition as our final authority in all matters of belief and conduct.

- The belief in the priesthood of all believers, which emphasized that all believers could have direct access to God without a priest acting as a go-between.

Calvin viewed what passed for Christianity in late mediaeval Europe as sub-Christian. He wrote boldly to a senior Cardinal in the Roman Catholic Church, Jacopo Sadoleto (1477-1547) in 1539: 'The light of the divine truth has been extinguished, the word of God buried, the virtue of Christ left in profound oblivion and the pastoral office subverted ... there is almost no divine worship untarnished by superstition.'[5]

---

4. 'A pathway into the Holy Scripture' in *The Works of William Tyndale* (Edinburgh: Banner of Truth, 2010).

5. Responding to an attempt by Cardinal Sadoleto in a letter written to

In re-emphasising these monumental truths, the Reformers sought to answer three central questions:

- *How can I be saved or made right with God?* Through the justifying and gracious work of God through Christ.

- *Where can I find my guidance for living and understanding God's purpose for my life?* How can I know what is true? What is my final authority for understanding God's purposes for me in the world? Pre-eminently through reading and understanding the teachings of Scripture which are above all, and ahead of any church tradition.

- *Can I gain access to God directly, without going through a priest?* All people have direct access to God through Christ, our great high priest, without needing the intervention of any earthly priest.

The Reformers summarised their central tenets in a series of '*solas*' (sole, or alone). At the heart of the gospel is a divine declaration that the righteousness of Christ is imputed to the believer because of God's grace alone *(sola gratia)*. Such justification is through faith alone *(sola fide)*, in Christ alone *(solus Christus)* and for the glory of God alone *(soli Deo gloria)*. The true record of this message is found in Scripture alone, which is the voice of God *(sola Scriptura)*. See Chapter 2.

THE IMPORTANCE OF BIBLES AND COMMENTARIES

Luther was a prolific writer. For a four-year period, in the early stages of the Reformation, he wrote the

---

secessionists in Geneva to return to the Roman Catholic Church.

equivalent of a two-hundred-page book every two weeks: commentaries, lectionaries and works of biblical theology.

Calvin produced his masterly *Institutes of the Christian Religion*[6] at the age of only twenty-seven. These *Institutes* are still widely-read, and used today in some of the most influential theological colleges in the French-speaking world as a basis for studying biblical theology and doctrine.

Others copied Luther's example, perhaps the most famous of whom was William Tyndale whom Melvyn Bragg regards as 'one of the greatest Englishmen'.[7] Just as Luther was the father of the German language, so Bragg and others argue that Tyndale was father of the English language. Bragg in fact argues that it would be impossible to understand Shakespeare without Tyndale, as Shakespeare quoted so frequently from Tyndale's text in his plays.

In a few short years in the 1530s Tyndale managed to translate most of the Bible from its original languages into an accurate and easy-to-read format. It was however illegal at that time to read the Bible in English in England, but he smuggled sixteen thousand copies into England before he was caught in 1535. So great was the excitement amongst its readers that some priests complained that people were reading the Bible aloud to each other even during the sermons.

Tyndale, like Luther, wanted the Word of God to be heard because he understood it to be the voice of

---

6. Hendrickson Publishers and others.

7. Melvyn Bragg, *Tyndale: A Very Brief History* (London: SPCK, 2018), p. ix.

God, and the truth of God to all the people. It provided comfort for the broken-hearted, light for those walking in darkness, a refuge for those seeking, forgiveness for those who felt under judgement. Previously the Scriptures were read aloud only in Latin and were often chained to pulpits in churches. Tyndale expressed his vision in striking terms, as to teach a ploughboy to read the Scriptures better than priests.[8] Nearly a hundred years later, in 1611, the King James Version of the Bible contained 93 per cent of Tyndale's translation.[9]

If we fast-forward to the nineteenth century, we see the forming of mission agencies and organisations such as the United Bible Society and Wycliffe Bible Translators. They worked with the objective of translating the Scriptures into the vernacular of indigenous peoples across the globe. All this had its roots in the commitment of Luther, Calvin and Tyndale to Scripture.

The Priesthood of all Believers

Luther had a revolutionary view of priesthood. His belief that all Christians are priests was based in part on 1 Peter 2:9, which speaks of Christians being a 'royal priesthood'. He thus argued that all followers of Christ had the ability to understand God's Word and were equal before God, and therefore that laymen could read and understand the Scriptures for themselves without the intervention of an ordained priest. He shared Tyndale's hope that the basic meaning of Scripture should be

---

8. See *Foxe's Book of Martyrs*, Abridged edition, Paul L. Maier and R. C. Linnenkugal (eds) (Grand Rapids, MI: Kregel Publications, 2016), pp. 269-270.

9. Bragg, p. 84.

understood by a ploughboy.

One genius of Protestant history has been to celebrate the unity and diversity of all God's people, and to glory in that diversity. Luther showed that through Christ, all believers had direct access to God, just as much as a priest had access, hence the term 'the priesthood of all believers'. God, he believed, was equally accessible to all faithful Christians, and all had equal potential to minister to others. He saw ordination as a pure invention of man and noted in his commentary on Galatians 1:15-17 the words of the Apostle Paul, 'When God called me to preach, I did not consult any man.'[10] There was no difference between peasant and priest—both had equal untrammelled access to God, with no mediator needed apart from Christ.

This had profound implications for the vocation of all human beings. We will return to this later. In his treatise on the New Testament in 1520 he further described all Christian men and women as priests and priestesses. For a sixteenth-century former monk, he had a particularly high view of women. We see this in his Epiphany sermon of 1528, where he dramatically assigns the title of 'preacheresses' to Mary and the other women who were the first witnesses of the Resurrected Christ: '… now these madwomen and fools became the first to whom Christ reveals his Resurrection—he made the same preacheresses and witnesses.'[11]

WORK AND VOCATION

Luther was convinced of the importance of vocation

---

10. Luther, *Commentary on Galatians.*

11. Luther, *Sermon for Epiphany*, 1528.

and calling for men and women alike in the world of work. Aristotle and Plato had believed that manual work was debasing and demeaning. The Latin word for vocation was understood by many to mean a call to the monastic life, leaving the world behind. But Luther wrote, 'There is no difference between the spiritual and temporal order. All Christians are to be priests and can exercise a calling in the everyday world.' The Reformers saw men and women as made in the image of God, as an expression of the 'imago Dei' in the world of work.[12] Our calling was not to leave the world behind, but to serve God in the world.

As a consequence, Luther sought to abolish the gap between priests and laity, and any implication that the priesthood was superior as a vocation. Commenting on Genesis 3:19, he wrote, 'What seem to be secular works are actually praise to God, representing an obedience which is all-pleasing to him.' William Tyndale subsequently wrote, 'While the washing of dishes and preaching of the Word of God represent different activities, as touching to please God, there is no essential difference.'[13] Later commentators like Vittorio Tranquilli demonstrated that both Luther and Calvin's theology led to a view of work as a dignified and beautiful means of honouring and praising God through His creation.[14]

Martin Luther King, over four centuries later, picked

---

12. See Gustav Wingren's *Luther, Lehre vom Beruf* (Munich: Kaiser Verlag, 1952).

13. McGrath, *Christianity's Dangerous Idea The Protestant Revolution – History from the 16th-21st Centuries* (London: SPCK, 2007) p. 337.

14. Vittorio Tranquilli, *Il Concetto di Lavoro da Aristotele a Calvino* (Milan: Ricciardi, 1979).

up this theme on a visit to Jamaica. On arriving in Kingston airport, he announced to his listeners, 'No work is insignificant. If it falls to you to be a street-sweeper, sweep the streets like Michaelangelo painted a picture; sweep the streets like Beethoven composed music; sweep the streets like Shakespeare wrote poetry … do it so well that the hosts of heaven have cause to pause and say, "This man was a great street-sweeper."'

So Luther and Calvin's theology had a remarkable impact on the world of work. No longer were followers of Christ called to leave the world, and many began to understand that they could serve God in the world, wherever He had placed them.

2

Looking at the Five *Solas*

The 'five *solas*' summarise the standing of the Christian as saved by grace alone, through faith alone, in Christ alone, as revealed through scripture alone, and for the glory of God alone.

Solas 1 and 2: Justification by Grace Alone Through Faith Alone

This doctrine is rediscovered in many of the great revivals in the history of the church. In this sense, the Reformation was also a revival. Subsequent revivals across Europe, in France under the Huguenots, in the U.K. under Wesley and Whitefield, in Norway under Hauge, and the series of revivals in Wales in the eighteenth and nineteenth centuries, as well as the New England revivals in the U.S.A., all had a rediscovery of justification by faith at the heart of their teaching.

Luther saw this doctrine as so central to the Christian message that 'it was the article of a standing or a falling church'.[1] If we are wrong in our understanding of our means of salvation, we will be wrong in our understanding of the character of God, of human nature, and of the role of good works in the Christian life.

Alister McGrath, in his well-researched and beautifully-written book *Christianity's Dangerous Idea*, commenting on Luther's sermon on good works, says, 'All Luther was saying was that good works are the natural *result* of having been justified, not the *cause* of being justified ... believers perform good works as an act of thankfulness to God for having been forgiven, rather than to entice God to forgive.'

Luther saw himself not so much as moving *away from* Rome, but moving *towards* the gospel.

LUTHER'S STRIKING PICTURE OF JUSTIFICATION

To help explain the meaning of justification, Luther wrote a short booklet entitled, *The Freedom of a Christian*. In it he described the good news of the Christian message as being like the story of a wealthy king, who marries a debt-ridden prostitute. The girl could never make herself queen, but the king loves her deeply, so on her wedding day, he makes a marriage vow to her. As a result of that vow, the prostitute becomes a queen. The King then covers all her debts and she shares his royal status and boundless wealth. She has not earned it; she did not become a queen by behaving like royalty. But the king, by his promise, has changed her status. She has experienced his grace, or sheer mercy. (The word 'grace'

---

1. Balthasar Meisner described the expression as a proverb of Luther (Anthropologia sacra disputation 24, Wittenberg: Johannes Germanus, 1520).

is an invention of the Scriptures to communicate God's boundless and undeserving love toward us.) The king is effectively saying to his new queen, 'I take you to be my wife. All that I am I give to you; all that I have I share with you.'

The new queen's response is the same response we are invited to give when God justifies us. 'There is nothing I can do to earn your favour; all that I am I give to you (my guilt and shame); all that I have I share with you.' In other words, Luther is showing that through the grace of God and the substitutionary death of Christ on the cross, His righteousness was imputed, or transferred to us, and our guilt was transferred to him. Standing before the God of all heaven, we appear in the righteousness of His Son. Christ bears our guilt and failure, and out of sheer love He now shares with us, who trust Him, all His righteousness, and life in all its fullness.

So, Luther writes of the new queen: 'Her sins cannot now destroy her since they are laid on Christ and swallowed up by him, and she has that righteousness now in Christ, her husband, which she may boast of as her own and say, "If I have sinned, yet my Christ, in whom I believe, has not sinned, and all his is mine, and all mine is his."'[2]

Sola 3: In Christ Alone

Some years ago, I was speaking in an open-air meeting in Sierra Leone in West Africa and attempting to convey the wonder of God's justifying grace in Christ. But I was using too much theological jargon. I had a very

---

2. Martin Luther, *The Freedom of a Christian*, 1520.

effective interpreter. After I finished – it took me several minutes – my interpreter simply declared to the crowd that, because of God's grace, 'God say, "Him, he okay!"' Everyone understood.

When the well-known twentieth-century evangelist, Michael Green, was travelling on one occasion in the Philippines, he was invited to speak in a prison. He wanted to explain the nature of God's justifying act. The listening prisoners looked down-at-heart and rather dishevelled, wearing their regular prison uniforms which were dirty. Michael Green himself was wearing a clean white surplice. As he came to the end of his talk, he wanted to make sure they would grasp the greatness of the gospel. Then he had an idea. He asked a prisoner to come forward and take off his prison shirt, while Michael took off his own clean white surplice. He put the dirty prison shirt on himself, emphasising that on the cross, Christ had taken on Himself our sin. Then he put on the prisoner his own beautifully-white clean surplice and explained that when we turn to Christ, Christ's righteousness is 'imputed' or transferred to us; so we are seen as clean before God, through this gracious act of Christ. The prison congregation apparently erupted with joy!

No wonder Luther himself, writing about this, wonderfully said, in effect, that if you knew what you were saved from, you would die of fear, but if you knew what you were saved for (communion with God, because of His justifying grace), you would die of joy.

SOLA 4: AS REVEALED THROUGH SCRIPTURE ALONE

When we read the Scriptures we are hearing the very voice of God. Luther argued that the Scriptures *are* the words of God, not that they contain, become, or express the words of God. Luther and Calvin went back to the sources of the Christian faith, that is the Scriptures, and they saw these were greater than the traditions of the Church Fathers. So today, evangelicals understand that the roots of their faith are found not in the Reformers but in the Scriptures. Luther saw that the purpose of the Bible was to reveal Christ. As Alec Ryrie, Professor of Church History in Durham University, writes, 'When the first generation of Protestants spoke of the authority of the Bible, this was understood to be the authority of the risen Christ, mediated and expressed through the Bible.'[3] Earlier, John Owen (1616-1683), Vice-Chancellor of Oxford University during the Protectorship of Oliver Cromwell, wrote of how we could know the Bible is God's Word, not because the Pope or some scholar tells us, but because God's Word proves itself to be true.[4]

It is because of this conviction that Luther, in the debate in the Imperial Court in Worms in 1521, memorably said, 'I am bound by the Scriptures I have quoted, and my conscience is captive to the word of God. I cannot and will not retract anything, since it is neither safe nor right to go against my conscience. I cannot do otherwise. Here I stand; may God help me.'

Believing the Bible to be the final arbiter and authority for our beliefs and actions, Luther committed himself to translating the Scriptures into the German vernacular.

---

3. Alec Ryrie, *Protestants: The Radicals Who Made the Modern World* (London: William Collins, 2017).

4. See Owen's defence of Scripture in his works: *The Divine Original of the Scripture* and *A Vindication of the Integrity and Purity of the Hebrew and Greek Text of the Scripture*. Both available online.

He translated the New Testament from the original Greek text in only eleven weeks, using much colourful and contemporary language. Because of this, many people view him as the father of the modern German language.

Sola 5: For the Glory of God Alone

It is God Himself who gives us grace to believe. We contribute nothing, and neither priests, nor bishops, nor even the pope can grant this. Calvin referred to God's grace in drawing people to Himself as 'irresistible'. The glory for the change in each life drawn into the kingdom of God must therefore go to God alone.

Reforming the World:
The Lordship of Christ

3

THE CHURCH AND THE WORLD

Luther's and Calvin's theology reformed and re-shaped the world. We cannot understand modern-day Europe without grasping its deeply-penetrating influence. These Reformers worked to apply biblical truth to every area of society. Neither Luther nor Calvin believed in a sacred/secular separation. They believed that the Lordship of Christ must be applied to every sphere of life, including the realm of ideas. One of their great disciples was Abraham Kuyper, a future founder of the Free University of Amsterdam, theologian and Prime Minister of the Netherlands. In 1880, he memorably wrote, 'In the total expanse of human life, there is not a single square centimetre of which Christ, who alone is sovereign, does not declare "That is mine"!'[1]

It can be argued that we lost our way in the church because somewhere from the mid-1800s onwards we retreated from engagement with society, and tried to

---

1. For more, read Kuyper's Stone lectures at Princeton Seminary, New Jersey, on the theme of how God's grace applies to religion, science, politics and art.

separate what we understood to be the Christian faith from its application to every sphere of life. This needs to be reversed.

The church has always struggled in relation to its view of the world. Our thinking has been governed by one of three broad approaches: (i) separation from the world; (ii) assimilation of the world into the church; (iii) engagement of the church with the world, resulting in both the transformation of individuals and society as a whole.

Let's look at these three in turn.

A. SEPARATION FROM THE WORLD

This was the dominant view before the Reformation, and has largely been the approach of the church throughout history. It is based on a wrong understanding of what it means for the Christian to be 'in the world, but not of it': that we are aliens in the world, existing, as it were, in parallel, but separate from the world with all its worldliness. The only way we can retain our purity is by cutting ourselves off from engagement with the world. In some ways this was the driving conviction behind the formation of monasteries, which provided centres to which believers could retreat.

This view is expressed in the famous classic written by Thomas à Kempis, *The Imitation of Christ*. The title goes on: '*and of Contempt of the World and All its Vanities*'. John Stott labelled this mindset as epitomising 'rabbit-hole Christianity'. The image is of a rabbit sticking its head out of its burrow to see if there are any enemies in sight. Then, when the way is clear, it races along the ground to search out a carrot or lettuce to eat, before swiftly returning to the safety of its burrow, unhindered, untouched and untarnished by the world around it. Similarly, some believers pop their heads out of their homes on a Sunday morning, walk hurriedly to church with a Bible under their arm, worship with others and then retreat to the safety of their homes without any connection to their culture. And at work or at college, they eat only with Christian friends at lunchtime. This may be a caricature, but it brings the point home.

Since the days of great social reformers like William Wilberforce and Lord Shaftesbury, we have tended to retreat from the world around us. This has led to unbelievers saying in effect, 'You are free to worship in your church buildings on Sunday, but keep your noses out of everyday issues in our culture, including the framing of laws, the world of politics, and the values of the weekday workplace.'

For many Christians, their faith is a private matter, and has little or no relevance to the wider world. They would struggle with the question of how to live out their beliefs in the workplace. Their attitude can raise doubts among younger entrants into the profession, persuading them to accept that their faith has little to say to the world of work.[2]

B. ASSIMILATION INTO THE WORLD

Behind this is the notion that if you can't beat them, you should join them—so that corruption, sexual malpractice, power plays have come to colour the institutional church, especially since the mid-1800s.

---

2. McGrath, pp. 313-18.

These all arise from a liberal view of Scripture. Before the Reformation, the church was rendered effete through the corruption of the papacy, but since the mid-1800s, liberalism has left the world bemused at the failure of the church to speak prophetically and distinctively.

C. ENGAGEMENT WITH THE WORLD

This third view has its theological roots in the doctrine of the Incarnation of Christ. When sent by His Father into the world, He did not require a space suit for protection, so He could separate Himself from the corruption, fallenness and brokenness of the world into which He came. He was the Son of God and also the Son of Man, and He became known as the 'friend of sinners'.

The challenge for many Christians who believe in separation is that we have no non-Christian friends. Yet we read in the gospel of John: 'As the Father has sent me, I am sending you.'[3] In working out how to retain our moral distinctiveness, we have tragically opted so often for remaining apart. 'The calling of the church and of Christians,' writes John Stott so beautifully, 'is to be morally distinct without being socially segregated.'[4]

Luther himself struggled with this issue, as we see in his view of the two kingdoms, setting private Christian ethics over against public morality, which was to be based on the force of the state. Calvin, however, emphasised engagement, while clearly retaining Christian identity. 'If the world is a wasteland,' wrote Alister McGrath,

---

3. John 20:21.

4. John Stott, commentary on Matthew 5: 13-14. 16 in *Through the Bible, Through the Year* (Oxford: Lion Hudson and Baker Books, 2006).

'the church is to be an oasis.'[5] This metaphor is worth our reflection. What can we, from our oasis, offer neighbours, colleagues, fellow students who live in the wasteland? Calvin uses a different metaphor, showing the need to maintain distinctiveness: 'We are to pass through this world,' he said, 'as though it were a foreign country, treating lightly all earthly things and declining to set our hearts on them.'[6]

---

5. McGrath, p. 322.

6. John Calvin, *The Geneva Catechism*, p. 145.

4

BECOMING A REFORMING AGENT

Let's look now at how Luther and Calvin sought to apply biblical principles in the world of the sixteenth century as reforming agents.

ECONOMICS

Under Roman Catholicism, the accumulation of capital was seen as intrinsically sinful. Money-lending for gain was not allowed, based on prohibitions given to the Jews in the Old Testament. Luther shared this traditional view, and in a sermon in 1524 stated that 'Christians should willingly and gladly lend their money without charge.'[1] He prohibited usury (money-lending for gain) based on Old Testament texts, as well as New Testament texts such as Luke 6:35: 'Lend to them without expecting to get anything back.'

Calvin offered a different perspective. In 1545, he wrote to his friend Claude de Sachin, 'Not all rules set out for the Jews in the Old Testament are binding on

---

1. Luther, Sermon in 1524.

all Christians … offering moral guidance only.'[2] As a consequence, Calvin broke new ground when he accepted the possibility of 10 per cent interest being charged on the lending of money. In so doing, he looked for the principle and purpose of the biblical prohibition, without focusing on the prohibition itself. So, he maintained, 'we ought not to judge usury according to a few passages of Scripture, but in accordance with the principle of equity.'

In so doing he was concerned to avoid the exploitation of power. This led Calvin to a significant shift in the whole area of money-lending and to the provision of variable interest rates. Some historians would say that this laid the foundation for the Swiss banking system! They have argued that money-lenders in the 1540s had bailed Calvin out with large loans when he faced financial challenges.[3] The German thinker Max Weber (1864-1920) linked the rise of capitalism to Calvinism, with its praise of virtues such as discipline and thrift as being good in God's sight.

It is interesting to compare income levels in Protestant and Catholic cultures, because of Calvin's teaching. In 1650 income levels in Protestant Netherlands were twice those of Roman Catholic Flanders, where traditional views of money-lending held sway. The Roman Catholic Church accepted the lending of money only from 1830.[4]

---

2. For perhaps the best treatment of this read André Biéler, *La Pensée Économique et Sociale de Calvin* (Geneva: Librairie de l'université, 1959), pp. 453-76.

3. See Martin Körner, *Solidarités Financières Suisses au XVIe Siècle: Contribution à l'histoire monétaire bancaire et financière de cantons suisses et des États voisins* (Lausanne: Payot, 1980).

4. McGrath, p. 334.

Some may have distaste for the capitalist system – and that distaste is justified in relation to its excesses – but moderate capitalism has brought many people out of the cycle of poverty.

An astute commentator on both capitalism and communism is Donald Hay, retired Professor of Economics in Oxford.[5] Hay reasons that while capitalism can underestimate the depth of human selfishness among the bourgeoisie, Marxism/Communism ignores the fallenness of the proletariat. The Scriptures teach that ' all have sinned and fall short of the glory of God', and the 'haves' and 'have nots' are no different in terms of the depth of their fallenness.

EDUCATION

Luther was converted as a young lecturer in the University of Wittenberg; Calvin while a student in the University of Orleans, southwest of Paris. It was through the universities that the Reformation spread across Europe: from Germany through the Netherlands, and on to Oxford and Cambridge, bringing Luther's and Calvin's ideas to England. Both contributed to the formation of universities and academies, and raised the level of education across central and northern Europe.

By 1552, Luther was Europe's most published author. One of his sermons at that time was entitled, 'On keeping children in school'. He strongly advocated the benefit of learning, given the wide availability of books, and the benefit of proceeding from school to university

---

5. Donald Hay, Grove Ethics series: 5a, *A Christian Critique of Capitalism* (1975); 5b, *A Christian Critique of Socialism* (1982) (Cambridge: Grove Books).

where 'one can learn more now in three years than was formerly possible in twenty'.[6] He asked the German princes to support the creation of more schools across German-speaking territories. Education, especially literary education, eventually became available to all.

By the late sixteenth century most German schools had boys and girls learning together. This compares favourably with what happened in Roman Catholic cultures. In Venice, for example, up to that time, nearly all students were male. As men and women are equal in the image of God, Luther wanted to see girls educated on an equal basis with boys.

Both Luther and Calvin were passionate, as we have seen, about translating the Bible; Calvin continued Luther's commitment to Bible translation with the production of the Geneva Bible, which is still used by many French-speakers today. In 1529, Luther's catechism established a Question and Answer format as normative.

In 1559, Calvin instituted the Geneva Academy to educate and equip many ministers, missionaries and others who would then permeate Swiss and French societies in a deep way. Other smaller but significant academies developed in Heidelberg, Germany; Leiden in the Netherlands; and Montauban in France.

Luther was very committed to family Bible reading and prayer as a means of educating family members. Later reformers would also focus on education in the family context: teaching, learning the catechism, and encouraging the reading of Scripture. Richard Baxter

---

6. From *Luther's Works*, Vol. 46 (Philadelphia: Fortress Press, 1967), pp. 213-57.

(1615-1691), a pastor in Kidderminster, England, urged a habit of family prayer. When he arrived in his parish in 1641 this was virtually non-existent. Nineteen years later, when he moved to London, family prayers took place in three hundred homes.

Robert Raikes founded the Sunday School Movement in the eighteenth century, which was the means, all across England and beyond, of educating many poorer people through learning to read Scripture.

The education of girls as well as boys created the seedbed for the emancipation of women in later centuries.[7] Luther went beyond this in his *Table-talk* when reflecting on human sexuality, to say: 'the marriage bed should be equally pleasurable for wives as for husbands'. This was an unusual view in sixteenth-century Europe where women were counted in law as the possession of their husbands.

As well, then, as bringing radical change to the church, the Reformation transformed and shaped the culture.

LIBERAL DEMOCRACY

Professor Robert Woodberry of the University of Singapore attributes the spread of liberal democracy to missionary endeavour.[8] He demonstrates historically and statistically, that what he calls 'Conversionary Protestants' (CPs) heavily influenced the rise and spread of stable democracy around the world.

---

7. See McGrath, pp. 339-43.

8. Robert D. Woodberry, 'The missionary roots of Liberal Democracy'. National University of Singapore, published in *American Political Science Review* (vol. 106., no. 2, May 2012).

CPs were a crucial catalyst in the spread of religious liberty, mass education, mass printing, newspapers, voluntary organisations and colonial reforms. Through these, the conditions were laid for a stable democracy to become more likely. His arguments are so powerful that it is worth summarising them.

First, the spread of liberal democracy is not a fruit of secular rationality, arising from the European Enlightenment; nor arising from urbanisation; nor from industrialisation. Rather, it comes from the influence of a biblical worldview, arising from the Reformation. John Locke (1632-1704) in England held to the idea of the equality of all people, an idea which has explicitly biblical and Reformation roots; similarly the values of Hugo Grotius (1583-1645) the towering Netherlands lawyer, theologian and diplomat. Benjamin Franklin (1706-1790) in the U.S. and Jean-Jacques Rousseau (1712-1778) developed what could be described as secular versions of Protestant and Puritan convictions and covenants.

Secondly, Protestant missionaries brought change. Missionaries were independent of the state, of slave-owners and of white settlers. This enabled them to defend the uneducated and the poor. In such ways democracy was gradually fostered, and the abuse of power was reduced, especially in relation to the slave-trade.

Methodists, Baptists and Quakers in the 18–19th centuries, often viewed as fanatics, led the campaign for the abolition of slavery. They saw that black people were made in the image of God just as white people. By contrast, in academic circles, black people were largely regarded as biologically inferior, so educating them beyond manual labour was useless.

Colonial governments, settlers and business people were generally wary of mass education. They preferred to deal with educated elites who would be easier to control, whereas missionaries argued for mass education. This was more pronounced in some parts of the world than others: for example, compare Francophone Africa with English-speaking Africa, where white Protestant missionaries were much more numerous and influential.

Third, stable democracies were born. These emerged first in Protestant countries, especially following World War 1. Democracy often lagged behind in Orthodox and Roman Catholic parts of Europe (as in Slovakia, Poland, Romania and Serbia) and in Latin America; and democratic systems have only become more firmly inaugurated in strong Catholic cultures since the 1970s, especially in Latin America.

After the fall of the Berlin Wall in 1989, countries in Eastern Europe with Protestant roots had more stable transitions out of Communism than those with eastern Orthodox or Muslim backgrounds, such as Bosnia, Albania, Romania and Serbia.

RELIGIOUS TOLERANCE

Further, some historians would maintain that the notion of religious toleration had its roots, in the first instance, in the Protestant Reformation and not in the Enlightenment, which came about one hundred and fifty or so years later.

We acknowledge, and we hang our head in shame at the religious wars which occurred in the 17th to 18th centuries. The Thirty Years War in Europe, for example, left four million people dead, for which we find no justification. It was, however, Oliver Cromwell in England who was the first Protestant leader anywhere to support religious toleration as a matter of principle. In fact, he invited Jews to England after centuries of exclusion. Even the historian Simon Schama, who is no great fan of Cromwell, expressed his gratitude to him for the acceptance of Jews back into England following the Putney debates in the 1640s. Cromwell even said he would have accepted Muslims if they wanted to come.

Now the notion of religious toleration in Europe is synonymous with pluralism and relativism. Cromwell had a stronger notion of toleration and would have understood the term differently. His view was based on the conviction that truth will always win out in the end. For him, toleration could be summarised as: 'I believe you should have the freedom to hold your own views. I tolerate that view and support your freedom to express it, but I believe your view is wrong.' The twenty-first century notion of toleration as expressed through a relativistic and pluralistic mindset, however, could be summarised as 'I believe this—you believe that. It doesn't matter; there are no absolutes—it's all the same in the end.'

As Cromwell believed the Christian worldview to be superior, and provided a good framework for living, he argued in favour of freedom for Protestant preachers and evangelists in England, alongside people who held different worldviews. He believed that as people heard different messages, the compelling truth and wonder of the gospel would be widely accepted.

MUSIC AND THE ARTS

5

LUTHER AND HYMNODY

Luther's theological convictions and his love of music came together as a means of communicating the freshness of his message. He was baptized in Eisenach in 1485 in the same church in which Johann Sebastian Bach would be baptized exactly 200 years later, in 1685. Luther even wrote a poem entitled *Frau Musiker* in affirmation of the beauty of music. He wrote the first Protestant songbook in Germany, with the help of his friend John Walter Torgal. He argued that we should both 'preach the gospel, and sing the gospel in schools', so that everyone could understand it.

From 1528 he made provision for four hours' teaching each week to boys and girls in Saxony, and he initiated the creation of adult music groups or singers in four-part harmonies, in every town. These lasted for fifty years. Women were allowed to sing for the first time together with men. The rich and poor were brought together to sing in congregations. Congregational singing replaced tenor soloists. He initiated special meals four times a year which provided beer for the singers. Luther's emphasis on singing was so profound that Diarmaid MacCulloch, Professor of Church History at Oxford, argued that it was 'the secret weapon of the Reformation'.[1]

But Luther's love of music wasn't shared by all the Reformers. Zwingli, in Zurich, was opposed to music. Calvin supported the singing of metrical psalms but was not enthusiastic about 'elaborate choral music which may stop you thinking about God'. Luther's revolutionary approach to music, however, could not be hindered, and it was picked up in subsequent generations, especially by the Moravians and by John Wesley, founder of the Methodist movement, who were the inheritors of Luther's vision for bringing music and theology together. On transatlantic voyages to the American colonies, Wesley and his fellow travellers would commonly sing songs on board ship. Bach argued,'Wherever there is pious music, there is always God's grace.' Martin Luther commented, 'Next to the word of God, the noble art of music is the greatest treasure in the world ... it deserves the highest praise. When people sing in four or five parts, it is like a square dance in Heaven.'[2]

Luther once expressed his desire for Christians 'to love and regard as worthy the lovely gift of music, which is a precious, worthy and costly treasure given to mankind by God'.[3] His fellow countryman, Bach, embodied a Lutheran theology of work, viewing all of

---

1. Lucy Winkett, BBC Radio broadcast, Sunday, 17 September 2017.

2. *Ibid.*

3. R. Bruce Elder, *In Harmony and Dissent* (Waterloo, Ontario: Wilfred Laurier University Press, 2010), p. 142.

his music, whether sacred hymns or secular cantatas, as a calling from God. As a consequence, he composed more than 1,100 chorales, passions, cantatas, and oratorios. Undeniably, Luther's ground-breaking movement – steeped in his dedication to promoting the priesthood of all believers – profoundly shaped Bach's eighteenth-century world. The Oxford University historian Bethan Jenkins believes that without Luther, there would have been no Bach.

So, Luther, Tyndale, Calvin and others had a profound impact on the theology of the church, the translation of the Scriptures into the vernacular, the development of modern European languages, and the nature of worship and music, both in churches and beyond, all across the continent of Europe. Their work would also bring the democratisation of education, the scientific method of enquiry, and a recognition that honest practice makes money. Their influence was profound, and we feel it today.

6

THE VISUAL ARTS, SCIENCE AND FAITH

Protestants have had an uneasy relationship with the arts, and an ambivalence towards the arts is still evident in some Christian traditions. We have seen how Luther – and Wesley two hundred years later – naturally embraced music as a means of expressing worship, of encouraging Christians, and of teaching doctrine. There was no sense of disconnection between spiritual truth and the swelling of song or of an orchestra.

Calvin was not in favour of images of God in churches; they were to be excluded. But he had a wide appreciation of other forms of art. He believed, for example, that painting and sculpture were permissible gifts of God. So he forbade the creation of artefacts to be worshipped, but not the creation of other works of art. Both Calvin and Luther wanted to reduce the status of the saints, and downgrade the centrality of relics, and this led some to engage in the destruction of artefacts.[1] It is important,

---

1. Protestants destroyed works of art from the Primitive Church of the first centuries onwards. This sprang from a fear that artefacts would encourage idolatry. So in a reaction to the theology behind

however, to see that opposition to artefacts, for both these Reformers, was primarily to the theology which the images represented.

In 1522, Luther wrote, 'I am not of the opinion that through the gospel all the arts should be banished and driven away, as some zealots want to make us believe, but I wish to see them all, especially music, in the service of Him who gave and created all of them.' Later, he wrote that 'it is better to paint pictures on walls of how God created the world ... than to paint shameless worldly things. Yes, would to God that I could persuade the rich and mighty that they would permit the whole Bible to be painted on houses on the inside and outside, so that all can see it.'[2] Similarly Calvin wrote that 'the invention of the arts is a gift of God, by no means to be despised'.[3]

So what can we learn from Reformation perspectives of visual culture?

Firstly, the Renaissance world of the fifteenth and sixteenth centuries was one where images were often idealised. Later artists, influenced by the Reformation, worked from the framework of creation, fall and redemption. Their gritty realism saw the messiness of

---

the images, icons were destroyed; walls were white-washed; statues were smashed. R. S. Thomas, a Welsh poet, declared Protestantism as 'the adroit castrator of art'. See 'The Minister' (1955) in *Selected Poems 1946-68* (Newcastle: Bloodaxe), 1986.

2. Quoted by William A. Dyrness, *Reformed Theology and Visual Culture. The Protestant Imagination from Calvin to Edwards* (Cambridge: Cambridge University Press, 2004), p. 54.

3. John Calvin, on Genesis 4:20, in *Commentary on Genesis* (Edinburgh: Banner of Truth, 1965), p. 217.

life.[4] The later French critic, André Félibien (1619-1695), writing in the mid-1600s, protested that the Dutch painters did not hesitate to depict nature 'with its defaults and not as it can be, in its purity'.[5] The Dutch painters' perception of the world was very different from the timeless, idyllic image of Italianate landscapes.

Assumptions about ideal beauty were being challenged and rejected. There was no need to represent an idealised Arcadia since the beauty and the wonder of God is manifest even in the most humble sand dune which holds back the mighty sea from swamping the low-lying Dutch polders. Such thinking was grounded in the new conviction that as God is the Creator of the whole earth, it was all worthy of study and representation.

This notion of 'broken beauty'[6] highlights the brokenness and fallenness of the world, and, too, the beauty of God's creation still reflected in surprising places, even in the midst of brokenness. A beautiful example of this is a portrait by Rembrandt (1606-1669) of his mother in the Rijksmuseum in Amsterdam, in which he paints her ageing hands and face with great care, including all her wrinkles and veins. Rembrandt shows in her both beauty and hope, especially through the use of light as it shone on his mother's face and on the Scriptures.

---

4. Over against the neo-platonic, idealised 'forms'. See Book 6 of Plato's *Republic*.

5. Cited in E. John Walford, *Jacob van Ruisdael* (New Haven, 1991), p. 15.

6. This argument is more fully fleshed out by John E. Walford, 'Broken beauty' in, Daniel Trier and Mark Husband (eds), *The Beauty of God: Theology and the Arts* (Downers Grove, IL: InterVarsity Press, 2006).

Secondly, artists influenced by the Reformation believed that all of life was worth painting. We see in their work not idealised religious figures, but landscapes, seascapes, flowers, shells, food and wine, as well as family life. These subjects expressed the conviction that all these things are created by God for us to enjoy richly, and are worthy of observation and admiration. Many of the early Reformed Dutch and German painters invited their viewers to see that in the midst of corruption, and despite the fallen state of mankind, there was beauty in all of creation. They brought together the fallenness and fragility of the world God had created, and its abiding beauty.

Prior to the Reformation, most European painters had been influenced by a Catholic cultural context. Samuel Escobar, the Latin American theologian and missiologist, points out that it was rare for Roman Catholic artists to paint the Resurrection of Jesus Christ, having an almost obsessive emphasis on the physical suffering of Christ on the cross. The Reformation, however, changed this and several Protestant-influenced painters such as Lukas Cranach (1472-1553), the German Lutheran painter, and Rembrandt depicted the Resurrection more frequently.[7] In so doing they highlighted the centrality of this event in Christian hope and the message the risen Christ offered to those who were broken, downcast and hopeless.

Many Protestant painters, especially those with a Dutch heritage, touched on big questions in their

---

7. See for example, *The Magdalen Altar*, Lukas Cranach 1520-1525, Stiftsmuseum, Aschaffenburg.

symbolic allusions to the brevity of life, the presence of God, and the hope of the gospel.

ARTS, SCIENCE AND FAITH

It is interesting to note that in the student world today most evangelical Christians are in the sciences, fewer in the humanities and the lowest numbers of all in the visual arts. This raises three questions for us:

1. Why is the gospel touching so few students of the visual arts?

2. How can we encourage Christians in the visual arts to apply their faith to their work?

3. How can we begin to communicate the word-based gospel message in a visually-saturated culture? Our response has often been to retreat from the visual, or to over-emphasise the word. We must find ways, like some of the sixteenth-century Protestant painters, to bring the two together. [8]

It is interesting to note that Protestant-influenced scientists saw no contradiction between their faith and their research. Richard Hooykaas, former Professor of the History of Science in the University of Utrecht, reveals that 'among the group of ten scientists who formed what was to become the Royal Society, seven

---

8. For further reading, see Hans Rookmaaker, *Modern Art and the Death of a Culture* (London, and Downers Grove, IL: IVP, 1970); Jeremy Begbie, *Towards a Theology of the Arts* (Edinburgh: T. and T. Clark, 1991); Calvin Seerveld, *Rainbows for the Fallen World* (Downside, 1980); Hilary Brand and Adrienne Chaplin, *Art & Soul: Signposts for Christians in the Arts* (Downers Grove, IL: IVP Academic 2001; Carlisle, UK: Piquant Editions, 2014).

were Puritan Protestants, thus taking their lead from Reformation thinkers. In 1663, sixty-two percent of members of the Royal Society were clearly Puritan in origin, the more striking because Puritans constituted a minority of the population.'[9]

Similarly, framers of the modern 'scientific method' saw no contradiction between their research, their worldview and Christian convictions. Johannes Kepler (1571-1630), the Lutheran Moravian astronomer, famously said that when he was engaged in his scientific research, he was simply 'thinking God's thoughts after Him'. Others included Robert Boyle (1627-1691), the founder of modern chemistry, and the Lutheran scientist Andreas Libavius (1550-1616) who wrote the first chemistry textbook.[10] To them it was absurd not to see God as present in everything. Some modern scientists have sought to separate scientific research from belief in a God who is there—but this was not part of the worldview of these early scientists. They would have concurred with the Belgic Confession (1561) that 'the universe is before our eyes like a beautiful book, in which all creatures, great and small, are as letters to help us ponder the invisible things of God'. The same conception of the Two Books and their parallelism is found in the work of the British natural philosopher and Member of Parliament, Francis Bacon (1561-1626).[11] We need to re-learn from their example.

---

9. R. Hooykaas, *Religion and the Rise of Modern Science* (Edinburgh: Scottish Academic Press, 1972) pp. 98-99.

10. McGrath, pp. 372-377.

11. Belgic Confession Article 2 and Francis Bacon, *The Advancement of Learning*, Book 1.VI (2).

RELATING THE GOSPEL TO LIFE

In summary, Luther and Calvin were instrumental in shaping modern Europe at many levels. They believed that the Scriptures had something to say about every sphere of life, including the realm of ideas. We impoverish the church and society to think or argue otherwise.

The Reformers, and leading Christian thinkers such as those we have mentioned, challenge us to reflect on how we can proclaim the great doctrine of Christian salvation, and apply biblical truth to every area of society and every sphere of life. God is interested not simply in the expansion of the gospel geographically, across the face of the world, but in the application of biblical values to every sphere of the world which He has created. Every good and perfect gift comes from above, and our God, the giver, is the Father of lights who does not change like shifting shadows (James 1:17). So let us seek both to appreciate all His gifts, and develop our understanding of them in the light of a God who has lovingly given us a framework for life.

In our churches we must teach the sovereignty and goodness of God over the whole of creation. Or we run the risk of impoverishing God's people and being unfaithful to the whole of the revelation of His purposes in Scripture. We also weaken our testimony to the God of the Bible before the watching world.

A Renewed Vision for Mission and Evangelism

7

THE RENEWAL OF THE MISSIONARY MANDATE

Leading missiologists and church historians have argued that Calvin and Luther showed little interest in cross-cultural mission and evangelism. However more careful recent scholarship demonstrates that nothing could be further from the truth.

Ralph Winter, an influential missiologist of the last half-century, asserted there were three great periods in the history of cross-cultural mission: the first from 1792 and the period following, with the influence of William Carey; the second from 1865, as a result of the ministry of James Hudson Taylor in China; the third from 1934, due to the influence of Cameron Townsend, who founded the Wycliffe Bible Translators, alongside the influence of Walter McGavran, the father of the Church Growth Movement.

Winter asserted that a fourth period occurred in the era following the Second World War, with the expansion of Protestant missions around the world.[1] This period

---

1. Ralph D. Winter, 'Four men, three eras, two transitions,' in *Perspectives on the World Christian Movement* (Pasadena, California: William Carey Library, 3rd edition, 2018), p. 34.

of expansion might also include the years following the fall of the Berlin Wall in 1989, as a result of which the evangelical church became genuinely global. Today, the largest number of evangelical Christians exist in the U.S.A., Nigeria, Brazil, India and in China. (In China alone there are perhaps a hundred-million evangelicals.) Since the fall of the Berlin Wall, and the opening of Eastern Europe, we have seen the birth and significant expansion of the church in other places, including Nepal, which has more than one million evangelicals; Mongolia, with over a hundred and fifty churches (whereas in 1990 there were only six known Mongolian believers); Algeria, in North Africa; Albania in eastern Europe; and Ethiopia.[2] Today, missions conferences regularly take place for students around the world, with large numbers attending in recent years in Nigeria, Kenya, Taiwan, Korea, Mexico and even Rwanda, as well as Europe and the U.S.A.

DIFFERING VIEWS OF THE YEARS FOLLOWING THE REFORMATION

In recent years, careful evangelical researchers have contended that the period following the birth of the Reformation (especially 1550 –1560s) was another age of vigorous and fast-moving expansion of the evangelical church.[3] One such, Fred Klooster, argues that the period

---

2. At the time of publication, Ethiopia has the largest IFES-linked student movement in the world, with over 45,000 students involved weekly in small groups.

3. Eg., see Michael A. G. Haykin and Jeffrey Robinson Jr., *To the Ends of the Earth: Calvin's Missional Vision and Legacy* (Wheaton, IL: Crossway, 2014); Jean Marc Berthoud, 'John Calvin and the spread

1555 to 1564 was 'perhaps the greatest home mission project since the Apostles'.[4]

This contrasts with Winter's view that 'Calvin did not even talk about mission outreach.'[5] The doyen of Anglican missiologists, Stephen Neill (1900-1984), writes in *The History of Christian Mission* (1964): 'There is no mention at all of mission in Calvin.'[6] Also the New Testament theologian A. M. Hunter (1906-1991), says, 'There is no trace of mission or evangelism in the *Institutes*.'[7] Scott Moreau, an American missiologist writing in 2004, claimed that Calvin said little about mission.[8]

Continental European missiologists are mostly in agreement with this perspective. Gustav Warneck (1834-1910) asserted, 'We miss in the Reformers not only missionary action, but even the idea of mission.'[9] This

---

of the Gospel in France' (a paper delivered at the Westminster Conference 1992, and published in *Westminster Conference 1992* by Reformation Heritage Books); Andrew Buckler, *Jean Calvin et la Mission de l'Église* (Lyon: Éditions Olivétan, 2008).

4. Fred Klooster, 'The Heidelberg Catechism and Calvin' in *Calvin Theological Journal* (Nov. 1972), p. 187.

5. Winter, 'The Kingdom Strikes Back', in *Perspectives on the World Christian Movement*, p. 18.

6. Stephen Neill, *A History of Christian Missions,* published as Vol. 6 of *The Penguin History of the Church*, 1990.

7. Quoted in Ray van Neste's article, 'John Calvin on Evangelism and Mission', *Founders Journal* 33 (Summer 1998), pp. 15-20.

8. A. Scott Moreau, Gary R. Corwin, Gary B. Mc Gee, *Introducing World Mission: A Biblical, Historical and Practical Survey* (Grand Rapids, MI: Baker, 2004), pp. 120-21.

9. G. Warneck, *History of Protestant Missions*, trans. G. Robson (Edinburgh: Oliphant, Anderson and Ferrier, 1906).

view was reflected in the planning of the 'Calvin 500' event in Geneva in 2017, to celebrate the 500th anniversary of Calvin's birth. Over fifty lectures and presentations were organised, but none focused on Calvin's vision for mission.

For the 500th anniversary of Luther's birth in the 1980s, in what was then East Germany, an installation had been commissioned of a large stained-glass window, with images of the twelve Reformers around Europe who were influenced by Calvin and Luther: from Italy, Hungary, Bohemia, England and the Nordic and Baltic countries. The Communist authorities saw missionary vision more clearly than Protestant historians! These startling and impressive windows include images of twelve Reformers influenced by Calvin and Luther, who took their teaching across Europe: Tausen (Denmark), Knox (Scotland), Cranmer (England), Olaus Petri (Sweden), Vermigli (Italy/Switzerland), Gaspard de Coligny (France), Michael Agricola (Finland), Stockel (Slovakia), Laski (Poland), Augusta (Bohemia), Honter (Transylvania), and Denai (Hungary). Together, they demonstrate the impressive reach of the Reformers' teaching across the Continent.

A MORE PROFOUND UNDERSTANDING

Johannes Verkuyl (1908-2001), the Dutch missiologist, brought a more subtle and profound understanding of the ministry of Calvin and Luther. In 1978 he wrote, 'It was easy to misunderstand Calvin's mission because there was little organisational structure in the church, which was born out of the Reformation.'[10]

---

10. Johannes Verkuyl, *Contemporary Missiology* (Grand Rapids, MI: Eerdmans, 1978), p. 19.

Before 1555, the Reformers were working to build structures for local churches which had seceded from the monolithic Roman Catholic Church. Few singularly Protestant churches existed at that time, though there were many home groups and informal Bible studies. These early congregations first needed proper organisation before they could think about evangelising the world. Once Calvin had brought some order to the Reformation, in the mid-1550s, rapid expansion occurred as missionaries poured out from Geneva all across Europe. Owen Chadwick (1916-2015), the Cambridge historian, writes that the problem for the Reformers was that, 'In breaking down papal authority, the Reformation seemed to have left the authority of Christian ministry vague and uncertain.'[11] In being loosely organised, there was a need for organisation in both structure and practice.

Much of the world outside Europe had not yet been discovered, including most of the Pacific Islands, much of Australia, the west coast of the Americas and most of Africa, apart from the Cape of Good Hope. Voyages of discovery had begun in the 1490s with great sailors such as Magellan, and Vasco Da Gama, but Europe was still viewed as the epicentre of the world, so the Reformers' minds were understandably focused, in the first instance, on their 'home' continent. In addition, the Roman Catholic nations of Spain and Portugal dominated the southern seaways and so prevented Protestant missionaries especially from making headway in Latin America.

---

11. Owen Chadwick, *The Penguin History of the Church: The Reformation* (London: Penguin UK, 1990).

We can, nevertheless, see missionary impulses from both Luther's and Calvin's ministry. Truth knows no boundaries, so while Luther was a passionate, even nationalistic German, his truth-claims of the Scriptures and the gospel had an impact way beyond Germany.

Luther's ideas crossed the North Sea, taking root in England, and the Nordic countries. In England they were first discussed in the universities of Oxford and Cambridge, and they would then spread to North America through the Puritan Fathers. Gripped by this new teaching, his followers took this fresh gospel message to the ends of Europe: the world as they knew it at the time.

The English Religious Settlement in 1558 was profoundly influenced and shaped by Lutheran convictions.

In his excellent article in Foundations magazine, Thorsten Prill challenges the traditional view of Luther's missiology. In the article he demonstrates that Luther's teaching gave birth to a huge missionary enterprise starting in Wittenberg. Hundreds of preachers went out from Wittenberg all over Europe. In addition to his many publications, and the translation of the Bible into the vernacular, these disciples of Luther, including Olaus Petra and Micaela Agricola to Sweden and Hans Tausen to Denmark, took this new or renewed gospel message all across Scandinavia and the Baltics as well as to the UK. Read this article to trace his missiology which gave birth to this missionary impetus.[12]

---

12. See Foundations magazine no. 73 autumn 2017, entitled 'Martin Luther and Evangelical Mission: Father or Failure?' by Thorsten Prill.

Let me briefly comment now on Calvin's theology, which shaped his action and his practice.

CALVIN'S THEOLOGICAL CONVICTIONS

Firstly, Calvin never penned a systematic treatment of his theology of mission. However, his *Institutes*, commentaries and letters contain many references both to his missionary convictions and missionary spirit. He clearly displayed a coherent theology of missions, based on at least four convictions: (i) a vision of the victorious advance of Christ and His kingdom; (ii) a passionate desire for God's glory; (iii) the doctrine of the 'open door' (see below); and (iv) his concern for the 'lost'.

Calvin's vision of the victorious advance of Christ's kingdom was pivotal in forming his thinking, as is clear in his *Institutes,* which he wrote when in his mid-twenties. He writes, 'God the Father has appointed Christ to rule from sea to sea and to the ends of the earth.'[13] Further, his commentaries both on Old and New Testament texts show how this theme runs through the Scriptures. In his commentary on Deuteronomy 33, for example, he writes 'We must, as much as in us lies, endeavour to draw all men on earth to Him.'[14] And commenting on the book of the prophet Micah, he writes that 'the kingdom of Christ has only begun in the world when God commends the gospel to be everywhere proclaimed, and at this day its course is not yet complete.'[15]

---

13. From opening dedication in the *Institutes* to Francis I. For a fuller treatment of Calvin and the kingdom of God, see Andrew Buckler, *Jean Calvin et la Mission de l'Église,* pp. 75-86.

14. Calvin, *Commentary on Deuteronomy.*

15. Calvin, *Commentary on Micah*, chapter 2, Verses 1-4.

Calvin's New Testament commentaries reaffirm this. On Acts 2 he comments on the coming of the Holy Spirit: 'The Holy Spirit descended in order that the gospel should reach all the ends and extremities of the earth.'[16] In addition, on 1 Timothy 2:5-6 he writes, 'Our Lord Jesus came to extend his grace not just to the few, but to people over all the world.'[17] On 1 Timothy 2:4 he states, 'No people and no rank is excluded from salvation, because God wishes that the gospel be proclaimed to all without exception.' He argued, 'God wants his grace to be known to all the world and he has commanded that his gospel be preached to all creatures. We must seek the salvation of those who today are strangers to the faith, who must not be deprived of God's goodness.'[18]

Calvin insisted it was the responsibility of all Christians to spread the gospel. He writes for example on Isaiah 12:5: 'For it is our duty to proclaim the goodness of God to every nation. ... The work is such as ought not to be concealed in a corner, but to be everywhere proclaimed.'[19] Moreover, he frequently makes use of Ephesians 2:14 to insist that 'the partition between the Jews and Gentiles has been broken down so that we, both Jews and Gentiles, have been gathered together into the body of the church and Christ's power is put forth to uphold and defend us.' This is so that Christ can be proclaimed as Messiah to the whole world. Calvin

---

16. Calvin, *Commentary on Acts*.

17. Calvin, *Commentary on 1 Timothy*.

18. *Ibid*.

19. Calvin, *Commentary on Isaiah* (Grand Rapids, MI: Baker, 1984) pp. 402-3.

frequently uses phrases like 'without exception', 'every nation', 'to all the world', and 'the extremities of the world'.

Secondly, a prominent thread running through the elaborate tapestry of Calvin's ministry and commentaries is his all-consuming *desire for God's glory*. For Calvin, it was the key motivating factor for world missions. When the gospel is proclaimed and accepted among the nations, God is glorified—which he saw as the chief end of man. Calvin's strong conviction about God's sovereignty over all things thus informed his attitude to the promotion of the gospel. His passion for God's glory was a deeply rooted motivation for the expansion of the gospel and the church over the entire globe. Commenting on Deuteronomy 33:18-19, he writes, 'When we know God as our Father, should we not desire that he be known as such by all ... and if we do not have this passion that all creatures do him homage, is it not a sign that his glory means little to us?'[20] Also, 'The whole world should be the theatre of His glory by the spread of the Gospel.'[21]

Thirdly, his theology was influenced by the doctrine of the 'open door'. We see this highlighted especially in his work on 2 Corinthians 2, and Colossians 4.[22] He writes, 'When the door is opened, so the servants of the Lord should make advances where there is opportunity .... Let us not withhold compliance with so kind an invitation from God.' He would have concurred with Augustine's

---

20. Calvin, *Commentary on Deuteronomy.*

21. Quoted by Samuel Zwemer. 'Calvinism and the Missionary Enterprise' in *Theology Today*, no 7, July 1950, pp. 206-16.

22. Calvin, *Commentary on 2 Corinthians* (see 2:12).

view of the open door, and Christian responsibility, 'Without God we cannot; but without us he will not.'[23] In other words, only God can open the door, but when He does so, it is our responsibility, as disciples of Christ, to go through it and to share the gospel freely as we are able.

Finally, his theology of mission is undergirded by his concern for the lost. The free offer of the gospel was not an embarrassment to him. In commenting on Micah 2:1-4 he writes, 'The Kingdom of Christ was only begun in the world when God commanded the gospel to be everywhere proclaimed, and to this day its course is not complete.' [24] On Deuteronomy 33 he writes, 'If we have any humanity in us and see men going to perdition, ought we not to be moved to pity to rescue the poor souls from hell and teach them the way of salvation ... a Christian who is not involved in mission is a contradiction in terms.'[25] Further, on Isaiah 2:3 he wrote: 'the godly will not be satisfied with his own calling and personal salvation but he will have a desire to draw others in with him.'[26] Again, commenting on the prophecy of Ezekiel, just before his death, we read, 'God certainly desires nothing more than for those who are perishing and rushing towards death to return to the way of safety. This is why the gospel is today proclaimed through the world.'[27]

---

23. Augustine of Hippo. As quoted in Robert Edward Luccock, *If God Be For Us: Sermons on the Gifts of the Gospel* (New York: Harper, 1954), p. 38.

24. Calvin, *Commentary on Micah.*

25. Calvin, *Commentary on Deuteronomy.*

26. Calvin, *Commentary on Isaiah.*

27. Calvin, *Commentary on Ezekiel* (see 18.23).

Calvin's theology of mission is God-centred and Christ-centred, focusing on the glory of God in Christ, as well as the duty of man. All life was to be lived for the glory of God. So Charles Cheney later wrote of him, 'The fact is that the glory of God was the prime motive in early Protestant missions and that it has played such a vital part in later missionary thought and activity can be traced directly to Calvin's theology.' It certainly had a significant influence on William Carey.

Some have stated Calvin's theology was a hindrance to missions throughout the sixteenth and seventeenth centuries, based on his understanding of the Great Commission and his doctrine of predestination. However, such accusations reflect a poor understanding of Calvin's theology.[28]

THE GREAT COMMISSION

Some have argued that Calvin believed Christ's so-called Great Commission (Matthew 28:18-20) was binding only on the first-century Apostles. But his reason for interpreting the Great Commission in this way was not to play down the necessity of cross-cultural missions in succeeding generations. Calvin was here fighting a battle against the Catholic doctrine of Apostolic Succession

His intention was to show that the Apostolate was temporary and ceased after the New Testament Apostles. The Great Commission was brought into this discussion to oppose Catholic practice, not missionary activity.

---

28. Scott J. Simmons, 'John Calvin and Missions: A Historical Study', pp. 4-6. Pdf available online at https://truthplace.files.wordpress.com/2013/01/john-calvin-and-missions-a-historical-survey.pdf (last accessed December 2020).

Indeed for Calvin, the Apostles only *began* the spread of the gospel to all nations. Earlier in his commentary on Matthew 24:19, he has written, 'The Lord commands the ministers of the gospel to go a distance in order to spread the doctrine of salvation to every part of the world.[29] ... the Pope ... and his band proudly boast of their succession, as if they held this rank in common with Peter and his companions, but ... no man can be a successor of the Apostles who does not devote his services to Christ in the preaching of the gospel.'[30] He made similar comments on other biblical texts.

Ruth Tucker, in her book *The History of Christian Missions*, argued that Calvin's doctrine of predestination 'made missions extraneous, if God had already chosen those whom he was going to save.'[31] However, Calvin insisted that the number of the elect is unknown and that therefore the gospel should be freely proclaimed to everyone. He drew on Augustine's teaching to support his view, which was 'for as we know not who belongs to the number of the predestined, or who does not belong, we ought to be so minded as to wish that all men be saved.'[32] In this way, the preaching of the gospel to the nations would not be hindered but encouraged.

---

29. Calvin, *Commentary on the Gospel of Matthew*, Chapter 28.

30. John Calvin, *Commentary on a Harmony of the Evangelists* (Grand Rapids, MI: Baker, 1984), pp. 383, 384.

31. Ruth Tucker, *From Jerusalem to Irian Jaya. A Biographical History of Christian Missions* (Grand Rapids, MI: Zondervan, 1983), p. 67.

32. John Calvin, *Institutes of the Christian Religion*, cf. 3.20.11, 12 and 3.23.14.

8

Calvin's Methodology

What most historians have missed in the debates about
Calvin's theology has been his astonishing creativity,
as well as his capacity to think and work strategically
for the advance of the gospel. He identified at least ten
approaches commissioned by God as means of getting
the gospel out within Europe, and from there to the ends
of the earth.

Systematic Preaching

Calvin would preach every day, morning and afternoon,
expounding the Old Testament on weekdays and
the New Testament on Sundays. He often preached
without notes, directly from the Hebrew and Greek. His
expositions were written down by scribes, which is how
his valuable commentaries came into being.

He insisted that God uses the preaching of the gospel
to bring people to faith. He wrote, 'Although God is able
to accomplish the secret work of his Holy Spirit without
any means or assistance, he has nevertheless ordained
outward preaching to use, as it were, as a means. But to

make such a means effective and fruitful, he inscribes in our hearts with his own finger those very words which he speaks in our ears, by the mouth of a human being.'[1]

One of his most striking comments on preaching comes in his commentary on Isaiah 12:4-5:

> As the Jews proclaimed among the Medes and Persians and other neighbouring nations the favour which had been shown to them, so when Christ was manifested, there ought to have been heralds to sound aloud the name of God *through every country in the world*; hence it is evident what is the desire which ought to be cherished among the godly—it is that the goodness of God may be known to all, that all may join in the same worship of God. We ought specially all to be inflamed with this desire as having been delivered from some alarming danger, and most of all having been delivered from the tyranny of the devil and everlasting death.

PRAYER

Calvin focused on the importance of *countless prayers* and wrote many prayers, especially for use during Sunday worship services. One example is the following:

> Moreover, we offer up prayers unto Thee, O most gracious God and most merciful Father, for all men in general, that as Thou art pleased to be acknowledged the Saviour of the whole human race by the redemption accomplished by Jesus Christ Thy Son, so those who are still strangers to the knowledge of Him, immersed in darkness and held captive by the ignorance of error,

---

1. John Calvin, ed. A.N.S. Lane, *The Bondage and Liberation of the Will* (Grand Rapids, MI: Baker, 1996), p. 215.

may, by the Holy Spirit shining upon them, and by Thy gospel sounding in their ears, be brought back to the right way of salvation, which consists in knowing Thee, the true God, and Jesus Christ, whom Thou hast sent.[2]

Corporate worship and intercessory prayer were central to the life of new congregations which came into existence under his ministry. A careful study of revivals throughout the church's history indicates that revivals have consistently been preceded by gatherings for earnest prayer. No revival has ever occurred without God raising up gifted preachers. In this sense, the Reformation both includes the reforming of the existent church as well as having some of the hallmarks of a revival movement.

DISSEMINATING SCRIPTURE

Both reformers, as we have noted, understood that the *dissemination of the Word of God* was central in the work of evangelisation, hence Luther's translation of the Scriptures into German, and Calvin's publication of the Geneva Bible. In the fifteen years before his death, Calvin helped with the establishment of thirty-four printing presses in Geneva, which poured out copies of the Bible in the vernacular, as well as much other literature.

It is easy to forget, in our contemporary world, that the Scriptures were so unread and unknown by ordinary people at that time. The translation of the Scriptures and their dissemination, as a result of the invention of the first printing press under John Gutenberg, played an

---

2. John Calvin, *Tracts and Treatises, Volume 2: The Doctrine and Worship of the Church* (Grand Rapids, MI: Eerdmans, 1958), p. 102.

immense role in the spread of the gospel message all across Europe.

PUBLICATION OF CHRISTIAN LITERATURE

Commentaries were needed to explain the meaning and application of the Biblical text. Both Calvin and Luther were indebted to Gutenberg whose press, like an internal combustion engine, propelled the gospel forth. While Geneva had a population of only twenty thousand, the publishing houses were printing three hundred thousand Christian books a year, carried by Christian colporteurs, at risk of their own lives, to other parts of Europe, most notably to France. These colporteurs were courageous men, not only preaching with courage, but making elaborate arrangements for their journeys. They travelled by foot through the Alps into France. The American historian Robert Kingdon (1927-2010) later investigated and found peasants who were still able to tell stories of the pastors of Geneva, the routes taken and their secret hiding places. The same routes taken by these early colporteurs were used later by the Resistance in the Second World War.[3]

EDUCATING AND EQUIPPING PASTORS AND MISSIONARIES

Seeing that Geneva had potential as a centre for evangelising surrounding countries, Calvin established the *Geneva Academy* in the 1550s. This would equip the growing body of pastors and train men for the ministry.

---

3. Robert N. Kingdon, *The Coming of the Wars of Religion 1555-63* (Geneva: Librairie. E. Droz, 1956), pp. 55-56.

More, it developed a reputation as a missionary training centre for ministry in Roman Catholic Europe. Calvin encouraged his students to read widely, and established a library for them in Geneva. Students often had rooms in the homes of professors, and learnt at their 'table talk'. Men served alongside their pastors for between one and three years in French-speaking Switzerland, in order to develop a sense of comradeship.

FOCUSING ON UNIVERSITY STUDENTS

Calvin targeted university students with the gospel. Few of the pastors came from the peasantry; most were well-educated, and the sons of noblemen. Training was provided in Greek, Latin and Hebrew from the mid-1550s. It emphasised character development, church history and systematic theology. By 1564, perhaps a thousand men had been trained through the Academy, not only for gospel work in Switzerland and beyond, but especially also for Calvin's own country of France.

From 1555 onwards, senior pastors met every Thursday in Geneva to organise the commissioning of men to France.[4] They looked carefully at the places asking for pastors – at the financial support; how many could be gathered at weekends – and carefully screened men for each area. They assessed potential pastors' strengths and weaknesses—for example, some could not be sent to large cities if their voices were not strong enough. They also evaluated whether these men had

---

4. Scott M. Manetsch, *Calvin's Company of Pastors: Pastoral Care of the Emerging Reformed Church, 1536-1609* (New York: Oxford University Press, 2012), p. 73.

sufficient boldness to preach with courage. They usually provided financial assistance.

Elaborate arrangement had to be made for the journey. They used aliases and often travelled as colporteurs through the Alps, carrying books at the bottom of their bags, with jewels on top, so that if they were stopped and searched, only the jewels would be seen and they would be allowed to pass. Some were discovered and summarily executed.

These young men were taught to mix with shoemakers and peasants. They would hold meetings in woods, as there was often antipathy to their message, and sometimes they suffered severe beatings. There is evidence that at least ten were martyred. Some of the routes they took through the Alps were used by French Resistance fighters in the Second World War.

Some of these pastors were recalled, as they were unable to stand the pressure; others returned for further training. Calvin seemed to make no distinction between church work and mission. He kept up an immense correspondence, writing letters to these pastors every day. This work was so impressive that the Anglican theologian Philip Edgecumbe Hughes (1915-1990) called Calvin 'the director of missions in the city of Geneva.'[5]

SHARPENING PUBLIC DIALOGUE

Calvin showed no shortage of courage, engaging in public dialogues—an often-forgotten art in our generation. He arrived in Geneva at the age of 27, persuaded to come

---

5. P. E. Hughes, J. H. Bratt (ed.), *John Calvin, Director of Missions: The Heritage of John Calvin* (Grand Rapids, MI: Eerdmans, 1973).

by the terrifying William Farel (1489-1565),[6] who was in many ways a mentor figure for Calvin. Not long after his arrival, the Roman Catholic priests at the nearby city of Lausanne were challenged to a public debate by the reformers.[7] Of 337 priests, only 174 arrived and, of those, only four had any ability to defend their doctrine. Farel and Pierre Viret (1511-1571), the great Swiss theologians of those times, were the spokesmen for the Reformers, and they took Calvin with them as an observer, as he had little experience of such debates. The debate went on for several days.

One priest, in defence of the doctrine of transubstantiation, started to quote from the Early Church Fathers. Farel and Viret were unable to respond effectively to this and looked to Calvin for help. Calvin proceeded to quote more passages from the Early Church Fathers from memory, giving the exact source in each case. It was an amazing display of learning which had an electrifying effect on the assembly. The opposition was dumbfounded. One priest was converted immediately and as a result of this dialogue, the city of Lausanne became Protestant and two hundred priests renounced their ministry in the Roman Catholic Church.

Luther, like Calvin, developed the pattern of engaging in public dialogues, especially with the Roman Catholic hierarchy. As ordinary people saw the Reformers defending biblical truth, they became persuaded of

---

6. Calvin wrote in the Introduction to his commentary on the Psalms that he was terrified when Farel seemed to accuse him of cowardice on his reluctance to return to Geneva.

7. Erroll Hulse, 'John Calvin and his Missionary Enterprise', *Reformation Today*, May/June, 1998, no. 163, pp. 11-15.

the truth claims of their message. This all has echoes of the perspective on the growth of the early church of the German theologian and historian Adolf Harnack (1851-1930). When asked why the church had grown so much in the centuries immediately following the New Testament era, he maintained that it was because the leaders of the early church 'out-lived and out-argued the unbelievers'.[8] This could equally be said of Luther and Calvin.

TARGETING KINGS, QUEENS AND PRINCES

Luther had brought a strategic mindset to targeting both educational institutions and the German Princes. Calvin, also a creative and strategic thinker, worked in a similar way.

Calvin was cautious about attacking magistrates or princely leaders. He was a good friend of John Knox (1514-1572), working in harness with him in the mid-1550s when Knox was an émigré in Geneva. But, unknown to Calvin, when Knox produced a pamphlet called 'The First Blast of the Trumpet against the Monstrous Regiment [rule] of Women' (1558) – opposing Mary Tudor's reign, and arguing that women rulers were contrary to God's law – Calvin saw the damage that the pamphlet could do to the Protestant cause; and banned its sale in Geneva. He was convinced that reform in Europe had to be brought about in the context of full submission to the proper authorities, which he saw as being ordained by God.

---

8. Adolf von Harnack, James Moffatt (trans.), *The Expansion of Christianity in the First Three Centuries* (Eugene, OR: Wipf and Stock, 1998).

When Elizabeth 1 was crowned in 1558, Calvin dedicated his commentary on Isaiah to the new queen in an attempt to mollify her anger at Knox's dismissal of the crown. But the damage was already done. In 1566, the French pastor theologian Theodore Beza (1519-1605) stated Elizabeth's hostility to Calvinism was as a result of this incident. Elizabeth's policy of adopting a 'via media' between Catholicism and Protestantism, aiming to strengthen the Anglican system of governors in the church, may have been a consequence of Knox's blast against female leaders.

Similarly, in France, the Renaissance King, Francis I, appeared to be open towards Protestants until William Farel supported the distribution of anti-Catholic posters around Paris, which became known as *Les Affaires Des Affiches* ('the affair of the posters'). This alienated Francis. Calvin was appalled, and in his *Institutes* pleaded for toleration of evangelical forms of Christianity. The aim of the *Institutes* was not to write a new systematic theology, but, as indicated in the Introduction, to provide a reasoned defence of authentic evangelical Christianity.

John Calvin wanted to see the peaceful advance of Protestant evangelical Christianity. Some suggest his efforts were hindered by the zealous but over-passionate hostility of some co-workers towards the Catholic church and their regal defenders. We cannot know the extent to which these divisions contributed to the wars of religion – The Thirty Years War in Europe (1618-1648) – which led to the deaths of four million people, as well as hostility towards, and persecution of, many Protestants in France, and across Europe.

In an attempt to build bridges with magistrates and rulers, it was a common practice for Calvin to dedicate his commentaries to Kings and Queens across the continent. One of his close friends, John à Lasco,[9] who spent time with him in Geneva, eventually returned to his native Poland where he found his king, Sigismund, to be a tolerant and enlightened Catholic who even had a Protestant wife. Calvin dedicated his commentary on the Book of Hebrews, published in 1559, to Sigismund, writing beautifully to him, 'Your kingdom is extensive and renowned, and abounds with many excellencies; but its happiness will only be solid when it adopts Christ as its chief ruler and governor. I, whom the King of Kings has appointed a preacher of the gospel and a minister of his church, call upon you, your Majesty, to make this work above all others your special care.'[10]

Unlike the fiery Knox, Calvin demonstrates a gentle manner in his style of persuasion and engagement with magistrates, Princes, Kings and Queens. On one occasion, he wrote, 'It would be better to die than to take up arms for the gospel.'[11] It was not his style to antagonise magistrates or rulers. In short, he was

---

9. Leading Reformer in Poland, a former priest, also a friend and former associate of Erasmus.

10. Williston Walker, *John Calvin: The Organiser of Reformed Protestantism 1509-1564* (New York: Knickerbocker Press, 1906), p. 385. See also Andy Buckler, *Jean Calvin et la Mission de l'Église*, pp. 177-198, for an excellent treatment of Calvin's surprisingly creative, open and engaging dialogue with princes, Kings, and political leaders. This was a key element of his strategy for accessing cultures with the gospel.

11. P. E. Hughes, 'John Calvin. Director of Missions' in *Columbia Theological Seminary Bulletin* No. 59.

concerned that a godly life and a gracious manner be present in unfolding, articulating and defending the Word of God.

EVIDENCE OF MISSION

One of the best evidences of Calvin's concern for missions is the *activity of the Genevan church* under his leadership. It became the hub of a vast missionary enterprise as well as a dynamic centre or nucleus from which the vital missionary vision it generated radiated out to the world. Protestant refugees from all over Europe fled to Geneva. They came not merely for their own safety, but also to learn from Calvin the doctrines of the Reformation, so that they could return home and spread the good news. Philip Edgecumbe Hughes notes that Geneva became a school for missions which had as one of its purposes 'to send out witnesses who would spread the teaching of the Reformation far and wide ....'[12]

So Geneva, a dynamic centre of missionary concern and activity, was an axis from which the light of the gospel radiated across Europe in testimony of those who, after thorough preparation in the school, were sent out in the service of Jesus Christ.

---

12. Ibid.

Growing International Influence

9

STRATEGIC INITIATIVES: FROM GENEVA TO THE WORLD

From about 1542 Calvin's Geneva had become a refugee centre for Protestants from across Europe. The number accelerated in the mid-1550s, many fleeing hostile rulers such as Mary Tudor. In a twenty-year period, the population of Geneva grew from around ten thousand to twenty thousand inhabitants.

Calvin was pleased to take in these refugees, though at times it was difficult to accommodate them. In 1551 he wrote, 'I am meanwhile much occupied with the foreigners who pass through this place in great numbers, or who have come here to live. ... [S]hould you pay us a visit next autumn, you will find our city considerably increased—a pleasing spectacle to me if they do not overwhelm me with their visits.'[1]

On one single day in 1557, eighty Protestant migrants arrived in Geneva, looking for help, of whom John Knox

---

1. G. R. Potter and M. Greengrass (eds), *John Calvin, Selected Works* (St Martin's Press, 1983), Vol. 6, Part 3. See also W. Stanford Reid, 'Calvin's Geneva: a Missionary Centre' in *The Reformed Theological Review*, No. 3 (Sep-Dec 1983).

was one. Geoffrey Elton, the Cambridge historian, described Knox's eventual return to Scotland, with a new passion for his country, as 'refreshed by springs from the fountain head'[2] and famously praying to his God, 'Give me Scotland, or I die'.

Calvin's Widening Influence

Through the evangelical writings produced by the printing presses of Geneva and elsewhere, the Reformed faith was exported widely in Latin, English, Dutch and French, as far as Poland and Hungary. Calvin fuelled and encouraged this new-found faith by his voluminous correspondence.

Calvin sent out his first missionaries in the early 1540s to Tournai, in what is present-day Belgium.

Calvin's friend, John à Lasco, who pioneered churches in London, Norway and Emden in Friesland in the Netherlands, was one of the most dynamic missionaries influenced by him. Before returning to Poland, à Lasco pastored a church in Frankfurt, which became known as the 'foreigners' church'. He spent the last few years of his life engaging with the rulers of Poland and Hungary in an attempt to persuade them to adopt the Reformed faith.

After à Lasco returned to Poland he busied himself in preaching, holding synods, stimulating the translation of the Bible into Polish, and seeking to draw the varieties of Protestantism into one church structure. Kenneth Scott Latourette, the great Yale church historian, wrote

---

2. See Geoffrey Elton, *Reformation Europe 1517-1559* (London: Harper Collins, 1963).

of him that he was 'an irenic soul who exerted himself on behalf of accord among the Protestants'. [3]

In 1554, Calvin sent the first reformed missionary to the Netherlands. Pierre Brully (c. 1518-1545) from Lorraine established a Reformed Church there but sadly was martyred after only three months. Guy De Bray, who had met Calvin in 1556 in Frankfurt, wrote the so-called Belgic Confession in 1559, which was subsequently published in Geneva in 1561. This Confession would become the foundation for the Reformed Church of Holland.

The Dutch subsequently produced missionaries of their own, largely through the writings of Hadrianus Saravia (1531-1613), who worked to develop a reformed missiology. His writings later influenced Dutch missionaries in India, such as Justus Heurnius. Missionaries were sent to India from the Netherlands nearly two hundred years before William Carey wrote his *Inquiry* in 1792. Saravia's work also influenced early Puritans in America, such as John Elliot, who worked amongst the American Indians in New England in the seventeenth century.[4]

The sixteenth century included the so-called 'voyages of discovery', when Magellan, Vasco Da Gama and Francis Drake were opening up the New World. While the Roman Catholic Church ruled the waves in the Atlantic, Calvin nevertheless made an attempt to send missionaries to Brazil. In 1550, the Reformed Church of

---

3. Kenneth Scott Latourette, *A History of the Expansion of Christianity: Reformation to Present* (Peabody, MA: Prince Press, 1975), pp. 793-794.

4. See Scott Simmons, pp. 12-17.

Geneva sent out two missionaries to accompany a group of French Huguenots hoping to start a colony in Brazil. They arrived in March 1557 and began work amongst the Tupinambas, an indigenous Brazilian people. The work was difficult and frustrating, and ultimately ended in disaster when the leader of the colony fell back into Catholicism. Several of the Huguenots ended up being martyred for their faith, not by the Tupinambas, but by their fellow Frenchmen. Only two were kept alive, because of their skills as a cook and a hairdresser!

Regardless of this tragic outcome, the effort is testimony to the fact that Calvin took action, both at home in the European context, and also further afield. The period 1555 to 1564 was remarkable for the number of missionaries sent out. Calvin wrote to Bullinger, 'It is unbelievable to see how impetuously our brothers are rushing forward. My door is besieged like that of a king. Vacant positions are fought over; our resources are exhausted; we are reduced to sending men with a smattering of doctrine.'[5]

The situation in Geneva had become more settled in the 1550s, so Calvin and his associates were able to concentrate on spreading the message of the gospel across Europe, but particularly in France, Calvin's home country.

THE PASTORS OF GENEVA
The pastors of Geneva met together regularly with Calvin, and kept occasional notes of their actions—this became

---

5. Quoted in Frederick Hodgson, 'The Evangelization of Mid 16th Century France', *Reformation Today*, January/February, 2008, 224, pp. 21-32.

known as 'the register of the company of the pastors',[6] which is perhaps the greatest source of information for the missionary activity in Geneva. In April 1555, for the first time, it listed the men sent out from Geneva 'to evangelise foreign parts'. It mentions that men had already been sent out to the Piedmont valleys, though more pastors may have been sent out before this time without being recorded in the register, as the notes were incomplete and it was perhaps dangerous to record actual names.

By 1557, it became normal practice for the Genevan pastors to send missionaries to France. Robert Kingdon called it 'a concentrated missionary effort'. By the early 1560s, the religious wars had broken out in France and it was no longer safe to record all the names of missionaries. However, the register records 88 men by name who were sent between 1555 and 1562. In 1561, even though the register mentions only twelve missionaries, other sources, according to Kingdon, indicate that at least one hundred and forty two were sent![7] Hundreds of men were being sent out to Scotland, England, Italy, Germany and much of France. Thus Geneva, under Calvin's direction, served as the heartbeat of the Reformation in Europe.

CHURCHES IN FRANCE

In 1555 the first organised or 'dressed' French reformed church, with its consistory of elders, deacons and established discipline, was formed in Paris with Jean Maco as pastor. Calvin made a distinction between

---

6. See Scott M. Manetsch, *Calvin's Company of Pastors*.

7. See Kingdon, *Geneva and the Coming Wars of Religion in France*.

'dressed' (formally constituted) churches, and planted churches, which were really small groups or nascent congregations. According to the French Protestant leader Admiral De Coligny, within seven years, that is by 1562, there were 2,150 dressed churches in France. These were often small and had to meet in secret, but were widespread across the country. Some, however, had become quite large. Pierre Viret, the close friend and co-worker of Farel and Calvin in exile, was preaching by 1561 to eight thousand communicants in Nimes, in the south of France. Berthoud describes the years of 1555 to 1562 as being notable for the 'unprecedented explosion both of conversions to the reformed faith and the establishment of formally-organised congregations'.[8]

By the time of his death, aged 55, in 1564, Calvin's influence over France had reached major proportions. There had been an explosion in the growth of Calvinistic congregations and influence, and complete reformation of France seemed a real possibility—perhaps one third of the nobility had signalled their acceptance of the new religious ideas. The Protestant churches had a total membership in excess of two million, out of a population of about twenty million. Many of these pastors were equipped first of all by Viret's academy in Lausanne as early as the 1530s, and then the academy which Calvin and his supporters set up in Geneva, backed by the venerable company of pastors.

Berthoud, quoting McGrath, writes that by 1561,

---

8. Jean-Marc Berthoud, 'John Calvin and the spread of the gospel in France', in *Fulfilling the Great Commission* (Westminster Conference Papers [London]: Westminster Conference, 1992), pp. 44-46.

'Geneva pastors were prone to disappear without warning, only to turn up in remote corners of France. Local Genevan parishes were stripped of their pastors in order to supply the burgeoning demand from French churches.'[9] It is no wonder that Fred Klooster has written that Calvin and his associates' commitment to mission and the evangelisation of France and beyond, during the period 1555-64, was 'the greatest home mission project since the Apostles'.

Calvin's statement that he was 'inflamed by a passion for the gospel' was clearly shared by many of his associates and the pastors. One has to ask why this missionary vision became more dimmed after Calvin's death in 1564. It is likely that the advance of the gospel was hindered because there was bickering and disagreement among Calvin's successors, and increasing hostility on the part of the French state and other nations.[10]

In the early 1550s, Charles IX of France pleaded with the Genevan authorities to bring back their preachers because the 'Genevan preachers are disturbing my kingdom'. By the late 1560s, however, consternation had turned to hostility, leading to the St Bartholomew's Day massacre in 1572: which resulted in the massacring of tens of thousands of Huguenot Christians, the scattering of Huguenots to the ends of Europe and beyond, and the re-assertion of the control of the Catholic-inspired state in France. One wonders what might have happened if religious freedom had been maintained for several more decades.

---

9. Ibid.

10. Robert Kingdon, p. 34.

The Legacy of Luther and Calvin

10

TEN LESSONS FOR TODAY

There is much to learn from Calvin and Luther about their vision for mission. Both reformers were strong patriots, with a love of their own culture and language. But they were more deeply captivated by the gospel—and the great truths of the Bible cross cultures and borders.

Luther's influence extended into the Baltic states, Scandinavia and beyond, and his teaching would leave a deep mark on the new Anglican church in England.

Calvin's theological awakening led to the advance of the gospel in Switzerland, all over the nation of France, and into the Netherlands, Poland, Hungary, and even as far as Brazil.

For these men, truth and mission were indissolubly linked, and the gospel they proclaimed was the focus of their preaching. Their creativity and strategic thinking are clear in the way they targeted university students, and engaged with Kings and Queens, and saw the benefit in working among the diaspora. They used literature; they worked in and encouraged Bible translation; and they were committed to church planting.

What then can we learn from their convictions and actions in the twenty-first century? Their ministry shaped the Europe we now know.

Churches and mission agencies could benefit from reflecting on the principles and convictions which guided them. I would like to suggest ten lessons we can learn.

1. THE IMPORTANCE OF BEING CLEAR ON THE GOSPEL

Both these Reformers thought the gospel was true, defensible, wonderful and powerful to transform lives and cultures. They believed the gospel was the greatest truth in the history of the world and it needed to be proclaimed in the public sphere. They were confident that its truth claims would win out over other worldviews. Perhaps the church, especially in Europe in the twentieth century, became too reticent to apply biblical truth in every domain, and retreated into the shadows, so we are regarded as having little to say.

Our message begins with the conviction that God became incarnate in the Person of Jesus Christ who died on the cross to pay the penalty for our sin and rose again to give us hope both in this life and beyond.

In addition, the Reformers fleshed out the need to apply the whole of biblical truth to every sphere of society, starting with devotion to Christ, then applying Scripture to every sphere of life. The Lausanne Movement, at its 2010 global congress in Cape Town, which brought together evangelical leaders from nearly two hundred countries, sought to build on this legacy in its *The Cape Town Commitment*, by calling the global church to 'bear witness to Jesus Christ and all his teaching—in every nation, in every sphere of society, and in the realm of ideas'.[1] We need to affirm robustly the uniqueness and truth of the Christian gospel, as well as the application of the whole of Scripture to every area of life. We have failed to challenge the tenets of secularism in the public sphere from the perspective of an all-embracing biblical worldview.

2. Motivation Coming from the Wonder of the Gospel

Our gospel is wonderful. Christ's teaching provides an ethical framework, the Cross demonstrates unconditional love, and the resurrection brings lasting hope. Luther's grasp of the wonder of the gospel is compelling: that if people knew what they were saved from, they would die of fear, but if they knew what they were saved for, they would die of joy.

If anything symbolises the western world today, and especially the European world, it is the loss of a sense of wonder about life in general, and in the church we see especially a loss of wonder at the gospel. We need to recapture that sense of wonder which the Reformers experienced, and identify with Calvin who said he was 'inflamed with a desire for the advance of the gospel'.

I well remember a conversation with Martyn Lloyd-Jones, the great Welsh preacher, while I was an undergraduate student. We were discussing the marks of great preaching. He thought there were three: the ability

---

1. J. E. M. Cameron (Ed.), *The Lausanne Legacy: Landmarks in Global Mission, Part lll* (Peabody, MA: Hendrickson Publishers, 2016), p. 102. See also pp. 163-172 for the author's 'Closing Address to the Congress'.

to communicate that the gospel is powerful, is true, and is wonderful. He sensed that the missing element in a lot of preaching is the failure to communicate the wonder of the gospel, something he so often did very well himself, with God's help. Perhaps we should pray for God to raise up preachers who are able to communicate their sense of wonder. It's easy to discern when this has happened, because then people do not say on their way out, 'That was a nice sermon, Pastor,' but rather, 'That was absolutely wonderful; it moved me and touched me deeply.'

3. THE POWER OF THE SCRIPTURES

It was a sense of the power of the Scriptures which energised the Reformers into translating and widely disseminating the Bible. Luther's work was especially influential in spurring on the translation of the Scriptures into many European languages. We need similarly to encourage the publication, dissemination, explanation and proclamation of the Scriptures as offering life-giving words, and speaking the 'voice of God' to our generation.

There has been a significant impact in universities across Europe in recent years through widely disseminating attractively-presented gospels followed by invitations to take a fresh look at the life of Christ. This 'gossiping of the gospel' alongside its public proclamation has provided a means, in God's hands, of many university students trusting Christ. This could prove an equally fruitful means of evangelism for churches.

4. Supporting proclamation with music

Music was a secret weapon of the Reformation. Word and song go together. As Luther said: 'Next to the word of God, music deserves the highest praise ... it is like a square dance in Heaven.'[2] We need to talk, preach and sing about God's good deeds to the watching world. Worshipful music opens the heart so that the proclaimed Word of God can take root.

5. Targeting the universities

In 1523, Luther said that if we wanted to change the world we needed to start with the university. There were only seven universities in German-speaking lands in 1500, but by Luther's death there were fifty, many of which began as a result of Luther's insistence on the value of education. Both Luther and Calvin believed in educating men and women. Luther in particular was egalitarian in his view of education. The Reformers contributed to the birth of many publishing houses—in Calvin's case at least thirty in Geneva that were pouring out over three hundred thousand books by 1560. Calvin set up his own academy, which was training over a thousand students in the year of his death in 1564. Calvin focused on the sons of the aristocracy to build his missionary force.

Both men were converted at university—Luther as a young professor in Wittenberg, and Calvin as an undergraduate in Orleans. In referring to his experience, Calvin wrote in his commentary on the Psalms, 'God, by a

---

2. From a presentation Lucy Winkett gave in a BBC Radio 4 programme on the Reformation, broadcast on Sunday, 17th September 1992.

sudden conversion subdued my heart to teachableness.'[3] Their message spread through the universities of Europe and especially, in England, the universities of Oxford and Cambridge. Similarly, today's church needs to focus on influential sectors of society such as universities, television, and media, to win the battle for truth in those theatres of influence.

6. WORKING IN TEAMS

Luther was surrounded by supportive princes and reformers: perhaps the chief of them was Melanchthon. Calvin was supported by Beza, Farel and Viret, together with his company of pastors in Geneva. John Donne was correct when he wrote, 'No man is an island'.[4] We need to be part of a supportive group. Christian leaders who are overly individualistic and 'shooting stars' will likely leave little long-term legacy. Both men were following the model of the Lord Jesus and the Apostles (and the women who served alongside them – see Luke 8:1-3) as well as the Apostle Paul, who mentions a catalogue of co-workers in Romans 16 (see also Phil. 4.1-3). They would both have agreed with John Wesley who later said, 'the Bible knows nothing of solitary religion. If we do not have fellowship, we must make it.' Christians in ministry should avoid falling into the trap of being overly individualistic and just ploughing their own furrow. Local, national and international networks help to extend the impact of the gospel.

---

3. John Calvin, Introduction to his *Commentary on the Psalms.*

4. John Donne, 'Meditation 17', from *Devotions upon Emergent Occasions,* 1624, later published as a poem in selected words from the prose meditation.

7. THE GOSPEL AND THE KINGDOM

Both these Reformers sought to apply biblical truth to every sphere of life, including the realm of ideas. They believed not only in the geographical expansion of the church but in the application of biblical truth to every sphere of life. This was picked up by some of the keenest of Calvin's successors, in particular by Abraham Kuyper of the Netherlands. Too often the church is guilty of retreating from society, as if we have nothing to say outside the church walls. This is a mistake. The Scriptures have something to say about every sphere of life. When we retreat from the world, we deny the Lordship of Christ over every sphere of life. We need to demonstrate how God's Word has application to all spheres of life: vocation, economics, political systems, art, science.

8. THE IMPORTANCE OF REACHING MIGRANTS

Migration is a cardinal issue in the twenty-first century. While unrestricted movement from one nation state to another can cause huge pressure on economies, education, health services and similar, it gives opportunity to reach people who can be difficult to reach in their own contexts. Calvin provided training for migrant believers. In recent days in Europe, we have seen significant numbers of Iranians, Afghans and Syrians trusting Christ. This seems to be one of the means which God uses to reach the nations. As we read the Acts of the Apostles, God shows us two strategies: (i) reaching people by sending missionaries to their cultures; and (ii) extracting people from their cultural roots in order that they hear the gospel. The Book of Acts shows how most people were converted away from their original home (see for example Chapters 2 and 8).

9. CREATIVITY IN COMMUNICATING THE GOSPEL
Printing presses of the sixteenth century were the equivalent of today's social media. Through using the technology of their day, the Reformers engaged in dialogue with their opponents. They sought to win over leaders with political authority, including German princes and European Kings and Queens. Calvin dedicated commentaries to magistrates, rulers and Kings, and corresponded with them. Luther was backed by the German princes. In addition, Luther used music to communicate the Christian message. Calvin set up an Academy for training. He made use of colporteurs. We need to reflect in a fresh way, as these men did, on Paul's injunction to seek to 'become all things to all people' (see 1 Corinthians 9: 19-23).

10. BELIEVING THE TRUTH ALWAYS SPREADS
Truth cannot be hindered by political boundaries. Ideas were spread from Wittenberg to other universities in Europe, and from Geneva to France, Scotland, England, Netherlands, Poland, Hungary, Brazil and elsewhere. The truth of the gospel cannot be contained. The Reformers' concern was not uniquely to understand and clarify the great truths of Scripture, but to propagate it to the ends of the earth (or to the ends of Europe specifically).

A TIME TO REFLECT
I have worked in student ministry in the European context for many years, and am often asked: 'How can

Europe be turned around?' or 'How can our secularised and multi-faith, materialistic continent be turned back again to trusting in the God of the Bible?' These are vital questions.

As God's vice-regents in this world, and with Scripture as our anchor, Kenneth Scott Latourette spoke of our having six weapons: prayer; evangelism; example; argument; action and suffering. Each was embraced by the Reformers, and we must lose none of them. For the gospel to permeate a nation, the 'action' and the 'argument' must extend deeply into the culture. This will require hard work and good minds. While the church is rightly concerned to maintain the centrality of Christ's saving work, and purity of doctrine, it has too easily neglected these aspects of our calling outside the religious sphere. The Reformers, as we have seen, did not neglect them.

Let us take time to reflect on the lives and legacy of these Reformers. Their example in the sixteenth century has much to teach us in the twenty-first. Our gospel is wonderful, powerful and true. May God strengthen our resolve as we, in our generation, work to bear witness to Jesus Christ and all His teaching—in every nation, in every sphere of society, and in the realm of ideas.

TIMELINE

This Timeline includes names of several leading figures from Europe who do not appear in the book. They will help to put the work of Luther and Calvin in context.

1320s John Wycliffe, 'Morning Star of the Reformation,' born in Yorkshire, England.

1372 Jan Hus born in Husinec, Bohemia.[1]

1384 John Wycliffe dies in Leicestershire, England. His challenge to contemporary beliefs is continued by a diffuse group known as the Wycliffites (or derisively Lollards).

1407 James Resby declared a 'heretik'. Burned in Perth, Scotland in 1407 or 1408.[2]

---

1. One-time Rector of the University of Prague, himself influenced by Wycliffe, and whose writing would influence Luther.

2. See the classic *The Story of the Scottish Reformation* by A. M. Renwick (Ross-shire: Christian Focus Publications, 2010).

1412 Jan Hus appeals publicly to Jesus Christ above church authority.[3]

1414 Jan Hus lured to Council of Constance.

1415 Jan Hus burned in Constance, Switzerland.

1416 Graduands at St Andrews University required to swear resistance to Lollards.

1433 Paul Craw (or Pavel Kravar) from Bohemia burned in St Andrews, Scotland.

1450 Johannes Gutenberg invents the printing press.

1466 Desiderius Erasmus born in Rotterdam, Netherlands.

1483 Martin Luther born in Eisleben, Saxony.

1484 Huldrych Zwingli born in Wildhaus, Switzerland.

1487 Hugh Latimer born in Leicestershire, England.

1489 Thomas Cranmer born in Nottinghamshire, England.

1494 William Tyndale born in Gloucestershire, England.

1491 Martin Bucer born in Sélestat, France.

1495 Thomas Bilney born in Norfolk, England.

1499 Peter Martyr Vermigli born in Florence, Italy and John à Lasco in Łask, Poland.

1500 Nicholas Ridley born in Northumberland, England.

1504 Heinrich Bullinger born in Aargau, Switzerland.

1505 Luther joins Augustinian monastery.

---

3. Marked the start of Bohemia's Reformation. Unnamed 'common men' were burned this year, probably the next-earliest martyrs. Over the course of the fifteenth century there was a spiritual dawn in several European countries. To borrow from Reformation scholar Heiko Oberman, the Reformation was the great harvest of the preceding centuries. Martin Luther himself was standing on the shoulders of giants.

1509 John Calvin born in Noyon, France.

1513 John Knox born in Haddington, Scotland.

1516 Erasmus publishes Greek New Testament.

1517 Luther posts 95 theses to door of Castle Church, Wittenberg.

1521 Diet of Worms. Luther taken into protective custody in Wartburg Castle, where he translates the New Testament into German. Henry VIII publishes his *Defence of the Seven Sacraments* against Luther and is awarded the title 'Defender of the Faith.'

1522 Luther completes German translation of the New Testament.

1526 William Tyndale's English New Testament completed.

1531 Thomas Bilney burned for heresy in Norwich, England.

1532 Thomas Cranmer consecrated as Archbishop of Canterbury.

1534 Henry VIII declared 'supreme head of the church in England'. First complete edition of Luther's translation of the Bible.

1536 Calvin arrives in Geneva. First edition of his *Institutes* published. Erasmus dies. William Tyndale executed.

1546 Luther dies in Eisleben, Germany.

1547 Henry VIII dies. Succeeded by his evangelical son, Edward VI.

1555 Nicholas Ridley and Hugh Latimer burned in Oxford.

1556 Thomas Cranmer burned in Oxford.

1558   Elizabeth I succeeds Mary, returning the Church of England to roughly its Edwardian state.

1560   John à Lasco dies in Pińczów, Poland.

1562   Peter Martyr Vermigli dies in Zurich, Switzerland.

1564   Calvin dies in Geneva, Switzerland.

1572   John Knox dies in Edinburgh, Scotland.

1575   Heinrich Bullinger dies in Zurich, Switzerland.

1611   King James Version (or Authorized Version) of the Bible completed.

1620   *Mayflower* sails from Plymouth to Massachusetts.

Appendix I

Confessional Statements Following the Start of the Reformation

These include:

Sixty-seven Articles of Ulrich Zwingli (1523)
Schleitheim Confession (1527)
Augsburg Confession (1530)
Genevan Confession (1536)
Belgic Confession (1561)
Heidelberg Catechism (1563)
Thirty-nine Articles of the Church of England (1571)
Canons of Dort (1619)
Westminster Confession (1647)
Second London Baptist Confession (1689)

Appendix II

Further Reading

Jean-Marc Berthoud, 'John Calvin and the spread of the gospel in France', in *Fulfilling the Great Commission* (Westminster Conference Papers [London]: Westminster Conference, 1992), pp. 44-46.

Melvyn Bragg, *Tyndale: A very brief history* (London: SPCK, 2018).

Andy Buckler, *Jean Calvin et la Mission de l'Église* (Olivétan, 2008).

J. E. M. Cameron (Ed.), *The Lausanne Legacy: Landmarks in Global Mission, Part lll* (Peabody, MA: Hendrickson Publishers, 2016).

Owen Chadwick, *The Penguin History of the Church: The Reformation* (London: Penguin UK, 1990).

William A. Dyrness, *Reformed Theology and Visual Culture. The Protestant Imagination from Calvin to Edwards* (Cambridge: Cambridge University Press, 2004).

Geoffrey Elton, *Reformation Europe 1517-1559* (London: Harper Collins, 1963).

Michael A. G. Haykin and Jeffrey Robinson Jr., *To the Ends of the Earth: Calvin's Missional Vision and Legacy* (Wheaton, IL: Crossway, 2014).

Adolf von Harnack, James Moffatt (trans.), *The Expansion of Christianity in the First Three Centuries* (Eugene, OR: Wipf and Stock, 1998).

Frederick Hodgson, 'The Evangelization of Mid-16th Century France', *Reformation Today*, January/February, 2008, 224, pp. 21-32.

R. Hooykaas, *Religion and the Rise of Modern Science* (Edinburgh: Scottish Academic Press, 1972).

P. E. Hughes, J. H. Bratt (ed.), *John Calvin, Director of Missions: The Heritage of John Calvin* (Grand Rapids, MI: Eerdmans, 1973).

Erroll Hulse, 'John Calvin and his Missionary Enterprise', *Reformation Today*, May/June, 1998, 163, pp. 11-15.

Robert Kingdon, *The Coming of the Wars of Religion 1555-63* (Geneva: Librairie. E. Droz 1956).

Kenneth Scott Latourette, *A History of the Expansion of Christianity: Reformation to Present* (Peabody, MA: Prince Press, 1975).

Scott M. Manetsch, *Calvin's Company of Pastors: Pastoral Care of the Emerging Reformed Church, 1536-1609* (New York: Oxford University Press, 2012).

Alister McGrath, *Christianity's Dangerous Idea: The Protestant Revolution—History from the 16th-21st Centuries* (London: SPCK, 2007).

Michael Reeves and John Stott, *The Reformation: What You Need to Know and Why* (Peabody, MA: Hendrickson Publishers, 2017).

Alec Ryrie, *Protestants: The Radicals Who Made the Modern World* (London: William Collins, 2017).

Scott J. Simmons, 'John Calvin and Missions: A Historical Study'. Pdf available online at https://truthplace.files.wordpress.com/2013/01/john-calvin-and-missions-a-historical-survey.pdf (last accessed December 2020).

G. Warneck, *History of Protestant Missions*, trans. G. Robson (Edinburgh: Oliphant, Anderson and Ferrier, 1906).

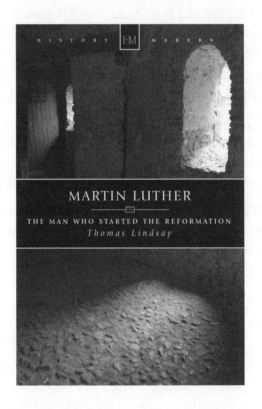

HISTORY HM MAKERS

MARTIN LUTHER

THE MAN WHO STARTED THE REFORMATION
Thomas Lindsay

ISBN: 978-1-85792-261-5

Martin Luther
The Man who Started the Reformation
Thomas Lindsay

- The father of the Reformation
- A passionate and courageous man
- Fought against the established church to bring about change

Martin Luther's father was a miner with ambitions - he wanted to better himself and provide his children with a good education. Martin upset his father's plan by becoming a monk rather than a lawyer, but by the age of 29 he was a professor of theology. In addition to his college duties he preached almost every day and visited people on pastoral duties - he kept two secretaries very busy.

Luther's father, meanwhile, became a town councillor, the part owner of six mines and owned a large house in the main street.

What happened to make this son of the upwardly mobile establishment into the revolutionary who nailed 95 Theses onto the church door at Wittenberg, affecting not only the whole of the Christian church but also breaking the power of a European superstate? This is the story of a passionate, flawed and courageous man who loved his family and the people around him; a man who went further in challenging the status quo than any other in history, the man who started the Reformation.

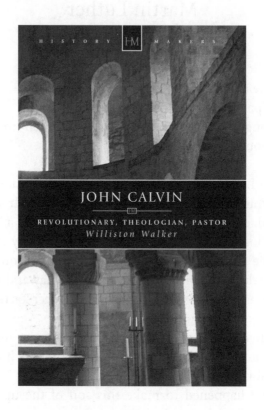

JOHN CALVIN

REVOLUTIONARY, THEOLOGIAN, PASTOR
Williston Walker

ISBN: 978-1-84550-104-4

John Calvin

Revolutionary, Theologian, Pastor
Williston Walker

- The great Reformation era figure
- Radically changed the face of Protestantism
- Calvin has done much to shape modern Western culture

Greater than any other Reformation era figure, John Calvin stimulated the debate, thoughts and ideas that have come to dominate Western culture and society. Dedicated to the reform of the church, and insistent on a literalistic reading of scripture, his influence radically changed the face of Protestantism and Society. Williston Walker produced this benchmark biography in 1906: it is still the best. Gripping, enlightening and authoritative – you will learn of a man whose theological stance and political philosophy has done much to shape modern Western culture and continues to influence millions of people in the 21st century.

Williston Walker was an American Church historian, born at Portland, Maine in 1860. He graduated at Amherst in 1883, and at the Hartford Theological Seminary in 1886, then studied at Leipzig.

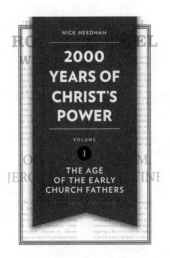

ISBN: 978-1-78191-778-7

2,000 Years of Christ's Power Vol. 1
The Age of the Early Church Fathers
Nick Needham

- Church History
- The Founding Fathers
- Explore the foundations of the world we live in today

Every generation has an uncanny tendency to view themselves as more enlightened than those that have gone before. The Church certainly has made mistakes all through history – and yet, no insights which we possess would be possible without the efforts, and even some of the mistakes, of our ancestors. The first volume of *2,000 Years of Christ's Power* covers the period from the 1st Century AD to the start of the Middle Ages. From the works of Saint Augustine of Hippo to the first apologetic ever penned, this time in history established the foundations of what we take for granted today.

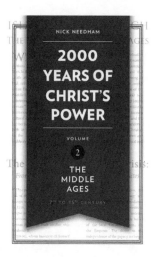

ISBN: 978-1-78191-779-4

2,000 Years of Christ's Power Vol. 2
The Middle Ages
Nick Needham

- Church History
- Middle Ages
- Path of Christ's kingdom before the Reformation

The Middle Ages were dubbed the 'Dark Ages' almost before they had begun to draw to a close. Ever since then, they have continued to be seen as a time of hardship and oppression, full of popes and crusades. In the second volume of *2,000 Years of Christ's Power,* another side of the Middle Ages shines through though: The continual workings of Christ as He built His kingdom through figures such as Thomas a Kempis and John Wycliffe, who lived and struggled during these centuries. This was far from a period of stagnation; rather it was the fire from which the Reformation was kindled.

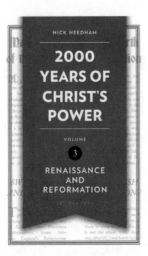

ISBN: 978-1-78191-780-0

2,000 Years of Christ's Power Vol. 3
Renaissance and Reformation
Nick Needham

- Church History
- Reformation
- One of the most exciting times of Christian history

The Renaissance was a reaction against the attitude of the Middle Ages. And the Reformation was the passionate, divisive argument that grew out of it. Catholics, Calvinists, Lutherans, Anabaptists – our present-day divisions were the front-page headlines of the Reformation. Volume three of *2,000 Years of Christ's Power,* in showing the progression of the Reformation era, and the daring bravery of its figures, presents a period of history from which there are many lessons to be learnt – not least of all, the vibrancy of people's lives and the courage with which they faced death.

ISBN: 978-1-78191-781-7

2,000 Years of Christ's Power Vol. 4
The Age of Religious Conflict
Nick Needham

- Church History
- 16th to 18th century
- Worldwide repercussions of the Reformation

The Renaissance and Reformation were exciting times of learning and discovery – they pushed the boundaries of accepted thought. The repercussions of this, however, were that they left in their wake a period of universal uncertainty. The centuries–old status quo had been turned on its head. Nothing was stable anymore. Conflict ensued. The fourth volume of *2,000 Years of Christ's Power* spans from the 16th to the 18th century. It presents a time from which English Protestantism, Scottish Presbyterianism, and French Catholicism, to name only a few, were birthed and refined. Perhaps few eras have had such a direct impact on the characteristics of our own period of history.

Christian Focus Publications

Our mission statement —

STAYING FAITHFUL

In dependence upon God we seek to impact the world through literature faithful to His infallible Word, the Bible. Our aim is to ensure that the Lord Jesus Christ is presented as the only hope to obtain forgiveness of sin, live a useful life and look forward to heaven with Him.

Our books are published in four imprints:

CHRISTIAN
FOCUS

Popular works including biographies, commentaries, basic doctrine and Christian living.

CHRISTIAN
HERITAGE

Books representing some of the best material from the rich heritage of the church.

MENTOR

Books written at a level suitable for Bible College and seminary students, pastors, and other serious readers. The imprint includes commentaries, doctrinal studies, examination of current issues and church history.

CF4•K

Children's books for quality Bible teaching and for all age groups: Sunday school curriculum, puzzle and activity books; personal and family devotional titles, biographies and inspirational stories — because you are never too young to know Jesus!

Christian Focus Publications Ltd,
Geanies House, Fearn, Ross-shire,
IV20 1TW, Scotland, United Kingdom.
www.christianfocus.com
blog.christianfocus.com